PLAYING BIG

A practical guide to forgetting your limitations and remembering the powerful person you are.

SCOTT ANDERSON

with MARK LANHAM

PLAYING BIG

The author gratefully acknowledges permission from Marianne Williamson to use a quotation ("You are a child of God; your playing small doesn't serve the world.") from her masterpiece, ***A Return to Love: Reflections on the Principles of "A Course in Miracles,"*** Copyright © 1992 by Marianne Williamson.

ISBN 978-0-9886526-0-6

DEDICATION

I am so grateful to my mentors and coaches who challenged me to Play Big including Click & Wilma Westin, Kevin Ross, Jeremy Stover and Eileen Blumenthal. Thanks especially to Marianne Williamson for her example and for the title of this book. I am also deeply appreciative of Carrie Duffy and Rasheen Coleman for their inspiring interviews, Fred Schott for his generous foreword, and Mark Lanham, my gifted writing partner, who Plays Bigger than anyone I know. Most of all, I am grateful to Sheila, my wife and best friend, and to my children, Grace, John, Max and Aidan, for their patience, love and support.

S.A.

TABLE OF CONTENTS

FOREWORD

I HOPE YOU'VE ALREADY BOUGHT THIS BOOK, but maybe you haven't. Maybe you're looking it over, trying to decide if it's worth the investment.

Playing Big is exciting but hard, even scary at times. The concepts presented in this book are very simple, but as Scott points out, there is a big difference between simple and easy.

As I write, I am a month shy of my 65th birthday. When I was younger, I could have used the wisdom, organization and exercises recommended throughout this short book. The discontent I experienced during the times I succumbed to fear and played small was debilitating and sapped my energy. On the other hand, I have tried to remember times I Played Big, and they were the times I was most scared. The stories and exercises contained here would have eased my mind, I'm sure.

I first met Scott Anderson, a talented young advertising and public relations professional, when we both served on the Board of Directors at the local Boys & Girls Clubs. At a strategic planning retreat, more than 10 years before he would crystallize his thinking into this book, Scott was Playing Big in his business and as a board member of this important non-profit organization. I'll never forget his challenge to us. "There are 50,000 kids in our city living in poverty and we are penetrating less than 10% of our market. We need to double our efforts!" Thus was born the 2X Campaign you'll read about in the book.

A large part of the Playing Big method is about taking the first step. Scott asks you to imagine doing for a living what you most enjoy doing, for free. Years ago, I was teaching a lot of parent education, practical tips on how to discipline, communicate with, and build self confidence in children—all for free. I started a business conducting parenting workshops before parenting was even a verb in the dictionary. It didn't go well because I played small due to my inability to price my services fairly. But that was just the first step. Three years later, I found myself building a career in the insurance industry. With my CEO's support, for over 20 years, I did more parenting and family life education programs across the country as an insurance executive than I would ever have done as a professional youth worker.

After the success of the 2X Campaign, I began to Play Bigger than ever. I resigned my job as senior vice president and chief marketing officer of the insurance company and returned to my roots as president and CEO of the Boys & Girls Clubs of the Midlands. I had more opportunities in the next nine years to Play Big than the previous 30. We more than doubled our impact and grew from three to eight locations. (One more was added a year after I retired.) It was a thrilling ride.

However, just as we were ready to open our eighth brand new Boys & Girls Club, the economic downturn occurred. I was afraid, terrified that what we had worked so hard to build would fall apart. But our board, staff, volunteers and donors all stepped up. They Played Big. In 2009, at the worst of the recession, our contributions exceeded our record year in 2008 by 46%. Our future was secure. Honestly, if you are a leader committed to Playing Big, you may just see your team, inspired by your vision, turn limitations into challenges.

In my case, Playing Big does not allow for retirement. It just means a new playing field, one that brings the freedom to dream even bigger. Over the next 20 years, I hope to be found Playing Big, bigger than ever. I want the next 20 years, or however long I have, to be the years in which I accomplish the most, when I have the greatest impact on the lives of children, especially poor children. Playing Big means I have to take the time to read Playing Big again ... and again ...

Do not buy this book and forget about it. Don't let it be forgotten on the bookshelf, or slowly buried in the pile of books on your nightstand, or floating in the cloud of your book queue. Take a deep breath. Read it. Keep it close and refer to it often as you start to Play Big. You will not be sorry. In fact, it could be the most exhilarating ride of your life, a life-altering ride.

Fred W. Schott, MS
Community Advisor President & CEO (retired)
Boys & Girls Clubs of the Midlands

INTRODUCTION

"You are a child of God; your playing small doesn't serve the world."
Marianne Williamson

HONESTY is usually a good first move, especially at the beginning of a relationship. The truth is, writing this book was one of the toughest things I've ever done. The thought of writing a book was terrifying, and one with such a lofty title—who did I think I was? I postponed the first meeting with my collaborator because of gut-churning fear. I made it to the next meeting because I was just as afraid to *not* write the book. So when you hear me extolling the benefits of Playing Big as this text unfolds, telling of the rewards it can bring you and those around you, know that when I started, I felt anything but big. That's one of the truisms I want you to know right up front—that feeling small is an early, and often inevitable, consequence of Playing Big.

But there's something that steadies me, and I believe it will steady you. In my initial shaky days, I came to a profound realization—that all the big things I had done in my life, the things that, in the end, really mattered to me—getting married, having kids, launching my business—all began with that same shaky feeling. Like at the outset, I'd been endowed with the original feet of clay, and to take even the first cautious steps toward my dreams would land me face down in inextricable mud. Each of those key ventures—proposing to my wife, having our first child, starting a program to help traumatized military families—all seemed to stretch my will, my faith, my finances and sometimes my sanity.

Looking back at those accomplishments, I see now that Playing Big is not just a way to maximize your gifts and leave a memorable mark in this life. It's the only way. If, as a culture, we're to move beyond our fears and really grasp the wheel and take the road less travelled, we have to be willing to stretch ourselves. As professional runners like Roger Bannister know, the first time is the toughest. Your hamstring strains to return to its accustomed posture. The next day it hurts, but the day after that, as you keep stretching, it gets a little easier—and then a little more. Finally, you're sprinting around the track in a way you could not have imagined a short time before.

Playing Big isn't about selfishness. It's about tapping into everything God gave you so you can make a better marriage, a better workplace, even a better world. It begins when you recognize that feeling small, standing with knocking knees at the edge of that grand precipice, is the very feeling that precedes great things. Marianne Williamson was right. Deep down, it's our greatness, not our smallness, which we most fear. Once you realize that and put that belief into action, you'll be amazed at what's possible—even in a short time. I'll show you how two of my proudest accomplishments got up and running in only 90 days.

Through it all, I've learned another important thing—that the capacity for Playing Big is not only for the gifted few. It's there for all of us. All you need is to get in touch with what you really want in this life and work a plan to get there. This book will help you do that.

Are you ready to stretch?

CHAPTER 1 – HOW TO PLAY

"They Laughed When I Sat Down
At the Piano
But When I Started to Play!"

John Caples

NOT EVERY PIECE of advertising is memorable, much less effective. But this headline, written in 1926 by John Caples for a U.S. School of Music mail-order ad, became one of the most famous pieces of copywriting of the 20th century. Not only was the ad successful in generating sales, but it also demonstrated how well its writer understood human nature.

Caples reveals a key insight here, one that largely explains why we're reluctant to play up to our true size: we fear the laughter. Picture that big piano—like the one onstage at Carnegie Hall—glossy, midnight black and as long as a tractor trailer. We're drawn by the mere sight of it. Every molecule of our being longs to slide onto the polished bench, to ease back the lid that covers the keys and bring our hands down on that regiment of ivory and ebony and produce glorious music.

We stand frozen, outside the spotlight that was meant for us because we're listening to a different track. You may know it well by now—that recording that plays over and over in your brain. It says things like "This is too big for you. You'll fall flat on your face. Stay small and you'll stay safe." And probably the worst one of all, "They'll laugh."

I offer you a fundamental truth: everyone is endowed at birth with the innate ability to Play Big. Your endowment for Playing Big isn't dependent on age, background, education, financial, marital or social status. It is your birthright. Watch young children at play. They play with abandon, without fear of judgement, inside that perfect circle where judgement is suspended, where laughter is the pure expression of joy, where the game never ends.

I'd also like to dispel an idea that may be brewing in your mind as you consider this concept—that what I call Playing Big is about puffing yourself up, exercising your machismo, a sort of W.W.T.D.? ("What Would Trump Do?") behavioral modification. Be assured that nothing is further from the truth. In practice, Playing Big is quite the opposite. When you're able to drop the pretense and connect with who you really are, the need for posturing disappears. Playing Big moves you into a world where you discover that humility and service to others are the true bolsters of your self-esteem and satisfaction.

So what happens? The simplistic answer is that we grow up. And there are advantages to becoming an adult, for the responsibilities we acquire along the way—higher education, family, a career—all demand a certain amount of maturity. But for most of us, at a certain point, our fear of 'not doing it right' begins to weigh us down. In the beginning, the fear is barely noticeable. One barnacle never sinks a ship. In time, however, if the fear that we're really missing the boat remains unchecked, it will pull us down. Eventually, we settle for the bottom when we could be on top of the world.

So Playing Big, to a big extent, is about detaching those things that have attached themselves to your surface, those largely untrue beliefs that have, over time, obscured who we really are. As I said before, the process of uncovering yourself is simple, but not easy. But here's the good news: everything inside you that allowed you to Play Big as a child is still intact. Think of it as that special software that was pre-loaded on your personal hard drive at birth. We only need to optimize that hard drive to get you up to speed.

I'm now going to take you through the initial exercise in my process for Playing Big. An important word before you begin, though. This exercise requires you to be completely honest with yourself. Frankly, I don't care what lies you've told yourself or others in the past—that you're just weeks away from the promotion that will change everything, that keeping a low profile is the way to get ahead or suffering is the only road to success. Just tell the truth here. Without a painfully candid assessment of where you are at this moment in time, the skyscraper we're going to erect will be built on a landfill, and the weight of your greatness cannot be supported on that kind of foundation.

The diagram on the following page is your Big Wheel. It encompasses everything you do, the segments that make up your life. When we were kids, it was largely a safe place to play. The most we had to fear was a scraped knee or elbow, but as we grew, those fears mounted; rather than being free within this wheel, we gradually became trapped by it, like the sole player outnumbered in an endless game of dodgeball. We're about to open this circle up again, to recreate that childhood space where it was possible for you to forget yourself and just be.

Notice that your Big Wheel is divided into eight segments: your Spirituality, Career, Money, Health, Relationships, Love Life, Growth, and yes, Fun. And if you wrinkled your brow at the "Fun" segment, you've definitely come to the right place.

Now notice that along the center grid is a scale of numbers from 1 to 10. What I'm asking of you, again with absolute honesty, is to rate your current satisfaction in each of these areas by drawing an arc along the number that best corresponds to your current satisfaction level. I urge you to determine your 1 to 10 ratings based on a typical day. For example, don't be tempted to rate your Career as a "10" on

THE BIG WHEEL

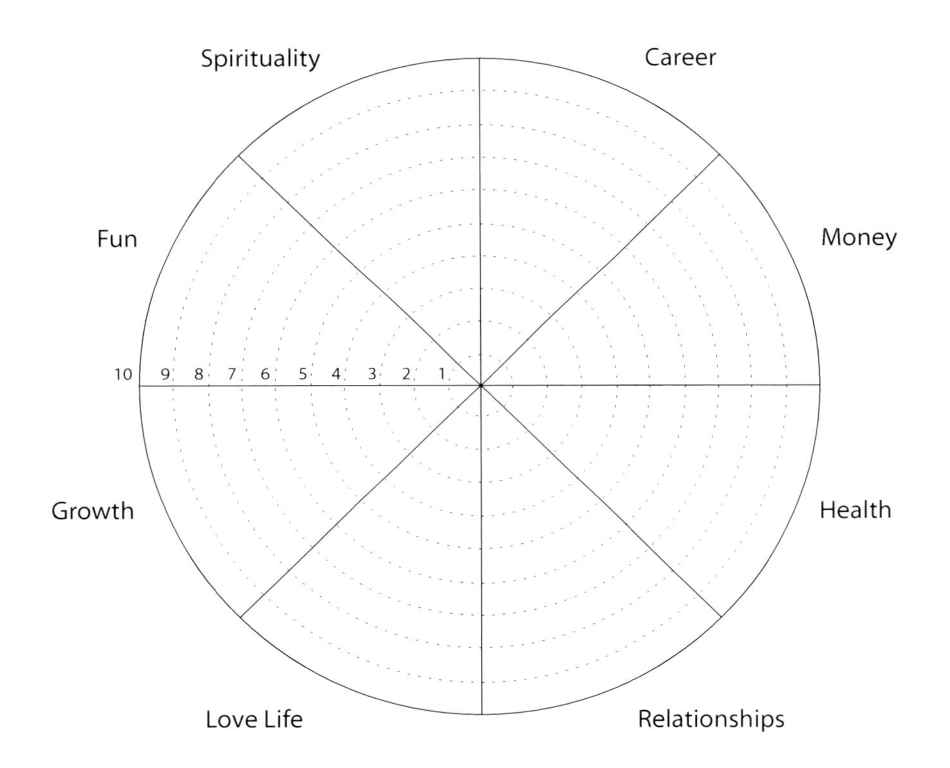

the one (and only) day out of 365 that your boss expressed his or her appreciation for your efforts. Again, be honest.

Be thinking as you score yourself, "What would it take—what changes might I need to make to raise my score from 2 to 4 points in any of these areas?" For example, if you're currently at a "6" in your career, what would it take to get you up to an "8"?

I'll describe each segment to get your mind going:

SPIRITUALITY—Do you have an understanding, or even just a curiosity, about a Power greater than yourself? What meaning does your "Higher Power" have for you? How close to or distant from this Power do you feel? Even if you are a member of a traditional religion or practice, would you like to expand your spiritual life? Or, is it very fulfilling as it is?

CAREER—I read one estimate that claims we spend nearly 100,000 hours of our life at work—and that doesn't include overtime. How satisfied are you on the job? Are you in your current job because that's where your passion lies, or are you just waiting and hoping for something better to come along?

MONEY—How satisfied are you with your financial situation? Are you able to take care of your obligations and still have something left to fuel your personal growth? Or is money a constant source of defeating stress?

HEALTH—Have you been to the doctor lately? Are you satisfied with your current state of health? Do you have all the energy you require to take on your daily tasks? And if you have any physical limitations, are you living fully within and around those 'givens'? How's your mental health?

RELATIONSHIPS—Is your life populated with loving, caring relationships with those closest to you? Or are there tensions, feelings of alienation, and a constant urge to skip going to Aunt Rosa's for Thanksgiving? Are there people in your inner circle to whom you could reveal your darkest secrets, free from the fear of being judged?

LOVE LIFE—Are you now with that special person? Still looking? With someone else but still looking? If you're in a long-term relationship with a spouse or significant other, how does that union feel? Exciting? Comfortable? Convenient?

GROWTH—Do you feel like you're expanding or contracting? Are you refueling yourself, opening up daily to new possibilities? Or do you feel stuck?

FUN—When is the last time you took a vacation? And were you able to actually enjoy it? In your current state, are you able to relax and just have fun, or does everything—including your down time—have to have objectives and a timeline? When was the last time you had fun?

As you rate your satisfaction in each segment, don't over-evaluate. While it's important to think this through, too much deliberation will muddy the result. Your heart knows the truth, you just have to have the courage to put it down on paper. Remember, this is for your eyes only—unless you choose to share it. Set time aside to do this exercise in one sitting. It's that important that you should not multitask this exercise with the other 17 things you've got going today.

Once you've completed rating each segment from 1 to 10, step back and review your work. Note the smoothness or bumpiness of your Big Wheel. If your circle were turned into the wheel of a car, how well would it roll down the road? Is it balanced? Where is your highest level of satisfaction? Your lowest? Are you rolling smoothly on the road of life, or do you see a broken axle in your future?

Here's a word of encouragement: wherever you find yourself today is the perfect place to begin Playing Big. You've just taken the most important step to getting on with your life in a bigger and more satisfying way. Assuming you've been honest, you now have an accurate take on how fulfilled you are in eight key segments of your life. Your courage is to be honored. This is the first step to Playing Big.

Let's go back to John Caples' famous headline, in particular the last half, "But When I Started to Play!" There's an important point here within the context of this ad. Caples was, in the end, selling music lessons. He knew that, unless you're a prodigy like Mozart, some training must come before Rachmaninoff will flow from your fingertips. The subsequent chapters of this book will guide you to take your rightful place at that big black piano.

If, up to this point, your life has seemed like nothing but work, get ready to play.

AUTHOR'S NOTE: At the end of each chapter, I've included a short list of suggestions called "Playing Bigger." These suggestions, built on the lessons of the chapter you've just read, offer you additional ways to integrate those lessons into your life.

PLAYING BIGGER

1. Take your completed Big Wheel to a copy center and have them blow it up—BIG. Post it in a special place in your work or home environment as you begin to live with it and focus on your goals.

2. Scan your Big Wheel and email it to your phone for easy reference when you're out and about.

3. Share your Big Wheel with a trusted friend. Tell them your goals. As we proceed, it will be very beneficial to have an accountability partner—someone you can check in with for honest feedback and support along the way.

4. Moving the Needle—Consider what level of satisfaction you really want in each area of your Big Wheel. Then begin to ask what steps you would need to take to get you from where you are now to where you want to be. For example, if you rated yourself a "4" in the area of MONEY, what would your life look like to be a "6"?

CHAPTER 2 – CAREER

"At the center of your being, you have the answer:
you know who you are and you know what you want."

Lao Tsu

ON MAY 6, 1954, British runner Roger Bannister did something remarkable: he ran the world's first sub-four-minute mile, breaking the long-standing mark with a record-setting time of 3 minutes and 59.4 seconds.

Bannister was a remarkable man. He began running at the age of 17. Blessed with natural athletic gifts and a competitive spirit, he never trained aggressively until his failure in the 1952 Olympics revealed what he'd need to do in order to achieve his goal. He upped his training regimen, and just two years later, he broke the world record.

On that historic May day at Iffley Road Track in Oxford, England, the wind was gusting up to 25 miles per hour, but Bannister was not afraid of a little headwind. In fact, in pursuit of his goal, he'd already been running in the face of a sufficient body of scientific opinion that what he was attempting simply couldn't be done—that the human body was not capable of such a feat. That if pushed to this extreme, his over-stressed heart would burst. It had never been done before. Therefore, it was deemed impossible.

A PROPHECY: Before we discuss this first critical piece of your Big Wheel, know that there are real consequences if you're choosing to play small in your career. In challenging economic times, the dangers can seem very real. Natural instinct pulls you toward equilibrium, to find that place far inland where you believe you'll be protected until it all blows over. Understand that you never go to that 'safe' place alone. Your entourage of coworkers, family and friends are dragged there with you, forcing this cadre you could be inspiring to hunker down beside you—costing both corporate and human growth. In other words, equating immobility with safety is a myth. Bannister put his head into the wind and ran.

It may ease your mind to know that if you're feeling stuck in regard to your career, you didn't get to that state overnight. In fact, homeostasis—the scientific term for our propensity to keep things on an even keel (aka being "stuck")—is part of our genetic coding. In other words, it goes down as deep as our very DNA. And eons ago, homeostasis definitely had its purpose. Consider for a moment your primitive ancestors. They had to survive day-to-day against a host of very real dangers that ranged from saber-toothed tigers to the unfriendly clan next door eyeing their spouse and supply of brontosaurus jerky. The very fact that you're sitting here today reading these words proves the effectiveness of homeostasis as a strategy for self-preservation—for telling you when to stay put and when to run like hell. A handy adaptation.

It kept your ancestors safe. It also kept them from taking the risks that may have brought them to greener pastures. But fast forward to modern times. Absent any real danger, your natural instinct to maintain equilibrium now has limited value, and is probably the chief trait that keeps you from Playing Big, not only in your career, but in every area of your life.

Consider this analogy: you know how your body has developed certain autoimmune responses that are triggered when they perceive a threat to the well-being of your organism? Your ego has done the same thing. The fear of failure, embarrassment, the laughter I spoke of in the previous chapter, all trigger inside you an automatic response geared toward protecting you from those fears. The ego's goal is survival at all costs, and the automatic response does not distinguish between real honest-to-God physical threats and those that exist only in your mind. So whether one is really stalking you or not, when your internal boy cries, "Wolf!" you run.

BEWARE THE LILLIPUTIANS!

It's time you met your Lilliputians. In Jonathan Swift's *Gulliver's Travels*, these tiny people—only six inches high—were capable en masse of tying down a fully grown man. Our fears do the same thing to us if we allow it. Think of all the little fears and misgivings that hold you at dead center in your career. Viewed individually, they don't stack up to much. But when enough of them accumulate, unquestioned, their effect seems quite powerful. And despite their Lilliputian proportions, they can effectively tie you down and immobilize you. It's not easy to Play Big when you can only move your limbs a fraction of an inch.

Look for symptoms that the Lilliputians are in control. Are you perpetually confused about what direction you should be taking in your career? Do you believe that you know the answers, but when pressed, your default response is, "I don't know?" When a career change is apparent, do you spend more time rolling around in the logistics than taking action—particularly if you believe that this change has a significant financial risk attached?

Here's the paradox: these Lilliputians are very real if you're unaware of their presence and potential impact. But once you recognize them, they can quickly fade back into the dusty pages of Swift's fantasy. Admitting that they're around you is the key to ensuring that you no longer have to live under their tiny tyranny.

Flip back now to the quote from Lao Tsu that opened this chapter.

Having consulted with thousands of clients, from CEOs of large corporations to small business entrepreneurs, it's clear that beneath the rationalizations and self-betrayal, they all know who they are and what they want. These are successful and highly functioning people who are often just stuck. When they think about what they really want, they easily get lost in the practical aspects of making a change—obstacles the Lilliputians love to roll into their paths to keep them where they are.

Our Lilliputians are most happy when we're immobilized between the rock and the hard place, where it's all black-and-white and you're stuck in a land of severely limited options. I've found that asking some fundamental questions can help you get unstuck—refocuses on your fundamental patterns and sets you up to start Playing Big in your career. Begin by asking yourself:

1. ***What would you do for free if you could?*** If you won the lottery tomorrow and money was no longer an issue, how would you spend your days?
2. ***Is there some work task in which you find complete absorption?*** You dig in, and the next thing you know it's three hours later and you've barely noticed the passage of time—it seems like minutes, not hours, have gone by.
3. ***What do you do in your free time?*** Is there an indicator here of where your real passion lies?

I'm confident that if you stop long enough to ask yourself these questions and are candid with your answers, you'll have taken a big leap toward discovering your true purpose.

As we go forward, you may discover that achieving the highest level of satisfaction in your career might only require a two- or three-degree correction to your current course. For example, I worked with a client recently who was a very successful commercial real estate broker, but she felt stuck in a passionless rut. I asked her what she would do for free if she could, and her immediate answer was raising horses. Her solution was to refocus her real estate sales skills into brokering farm and ranch properties. Now she earns her daily bread in an environment and with people where she feels most authentic. It's a wonderful example that contradicts our conditioning that we can never have our cake and eat it, too.

I give her a lot of credit. Playing Big is not without its risks. It took a huge leap of faith, turning away from her six-figure income and in the direction of her true purpose. But beyond the fears was a payoff that was bigger than money. Read her inspiring story on page 78.

Playing Big may not require a career change at all, but it almost always requires a fundamental change in how you approach your career. The road to complete satisfaction will demand that you evaluate your current mind-set and how you bring yourself into the brave new world you're about to occupy.

You've answered the questions. You've said out loud who you are and what you want. Now I want to give you three practical steps that will become important guideposts as you move forward.

1. Channeling—You've always had heroes, probably since you were a kid. Is there someone you admire that can serve as your spiritual mentor, a person whose talent, drive and integrity can act as your personal lighthouse? In my case, and particularly for the writing of this book, it is Marianne Williamson, noted author and spiritual activist. I can still remember the impact that her first book, *A Return to Love*, made on me more than 25 years ago. Since then, she has been a continuous source of inspiration and motivation, always in the background urging me to Play Big in moments when my Lilliputians are tightening their tie ropes. Often when I'm at a crossroads and need direction, simply asking myself, "What would Marianne Williamson do?" provides an immediate and powerful answer.

2. Getting Into Character—Every good actor has a process for getting into character, for assuming the role he or she has been hired to play. For the most gifted performers, the process produces such a complete transformation that after the show, again in street clothes, you may fail to recognize that actor as he exits via the backstage door. I've seen the same transformation happen in so many cases with my clients when they begin to embody the qualities of their heroes. This isn't about pretending to be someone you're not. Rather, it's using that special person to access those same qualities that are also in you. A number of times during the writing of this book, I was able to imagine what kind of a pep talk Marianne Williamson might give to keep moving forward. As you practice this technique, you will have moments when you'll look in the mirror and wonder at the aliveness you see in that person staring back at you. This tool can be especially useful if you're trying on the wings of leadership for the first time.
3. Working your Wheel—Assuming you've done the exercise and rated your career satisfaction from 1 to 10, we're ready to look deeper. Now it's just a question of how far you want to reach and how fast you want to go. Ask yourself:
   A) *"Where are you today?"* What's your current level of satisfaction in your career? And remember, take an average day, not that rare day you get the pat on the back that's supposed to make it all worthwhile. Let's say for the sake of this illustration that you're at a "4."
   B) *"What would it feel like to be at 10"?* Imagine that your career satisfaction level were at the top of the scale. Slip it on—like a new, custom-tailored suit. How does it feel? Does it change the attitudes and beliefs you currently hold about yourself and your life?

C) *"What would my career look like at 10?"* Specifically, what you would do all day? With whom? Visualize it. What does it look like?

D) *"What will it take?"* You identified where you're at now. You then imagined what total satisfaction feels like. Now I'm asking you to think about what it would take to move from your current state of "4" to, let's say an "8." And just like you knew the answer to the other questions, you already know what it will take. Make a list of what's necessary to move your needle to the right. Whatever it is—additional skills, contacts, cash—write it down. You've just created your own specific action plan for Playing Big in your career. For my clients, knowing that they're capable of charting a pragmatic course to increase their career satisfaction is incredibly empowering.

4. Your Ally—One of the most important parts of fulfilling the plan you just created involves collaborating with what I call an *ally.* I serve in this capacity for the clients I coach, and I also have an ally of my own that keeps me on track. You can hire your own coach, or there may be someone in your life already who could take this role. When making this crucial alliance, you must choose someone you can be completely honest with, and who will offer you the same honesty in return. This isn't about finding a "feel good" partner that lulls you to sleep. Rather, this person should be your ongoing wake-up call, testing what you've said you'll do against what you're actually accomplishing. There are several important benefits to collaborating with your ally:

   A) *Focus*—Your ally stands as a lookout for the Lilliputians, signaling you when they begin to dominate your thinking and downsize your possibilities. He or she also functions as your automatic pilot, alerting you when you drift off course and need to return to the original flight plan.

B) *Accountability*—You need someone to report to, to make you responsible for doing what you say you'll do and, most importantly, noting when you don't. I find this is particularly helpful among my clients who are CEOs and leaders in their firms. When the boss gets a boss, things get done.

C) *Challenge*—Your third-party ally should fully believe in your potential and challenge you to realize your potential to Play Big. Your ally should not be afraid to remind you of your commitment to Play Big, and to point out when you settle for less.

The law of inertia states that objects at rest remain at rest absent of outside force. If your career is in a state of inertia, applying force with the tools I've outlined in this chapter can change the course of your life, making a profound impact on the way you feel every day when you get up and go to work. Remember that statistic? 100,000 hours of your life are spent at work. In a state of inertia, it could well feel like 300,000 hours—or more! Or it could feel like seconds when you start Playing Big and letting it flow.

Here's one last bit about Roger Bannister. Only a month and a half after he broke the four-minute-mile record, other runners around the world began to break it, too. Bannister's courage has inspired generations of athletes to reach beyond the "known"—to trust what is in their hearts, to wave at the Lilliputians along the side but keep on running. The most powerful part of this story and its implications on Playing Big lies in a couple of simple stats. It took 19 years to break the four-minute-mile record. Yet once that record fell, it took less than 60 days before it was broken again—and then continued to be broken by many more runners in short succession. One man showed us what was possible, and a much bigger wave of achievement followed in his wake.

Incidentally, the first man to best Bannister's new record was an Australian named John Landy. But Bannister wasn't finished. In August of 1954, Landy and Bannister raced against each other in Vancouver, and Bannister beat his Aussie rival with a winning time of 3 minutes, 58.8 seconds. A larger-than-life bronze statue of the pair was erected to mark the occasion.

How big will your statue be?

PLAYING BIGGER:

1. Get a photo or other visual representation of the hero you intend to channel. Put it somewhere you can see it throughout your day.

2. Read a biography of the person you want to channel. If none is available, write one yourself.

3. Make a comprehensive list of those things you need to move your career satisfaction from where it is now up to a "10."

4. Meet with your third-party ally. Decide the best time to check in on a regular basis. Choose a good locale and format for those meetings. Keep notes. Be accountable. Ask your ally to hold your feet to the fire.

5. Make mental or actual note of when the Lilliputians come up throughout your work day. Work with your ally to develop a list of actions that most effectively drive your Lilliputians away.

6. Your success depends on focus. Focus instantly on the "what" you want. The "how" will appear. It really will. Write down what you really want and review it with your ally. Is there a way to state it that is clearer, more honest, more from the heart?

CHAPTER 3 – MONEY

"Your life is worth much more than gold."

from "Jamming," by Bob Marley

THERE'S A PHENOMENON taking place today in an isolated corner of northeastern Nevada that hearkens back to the glory days of the American Wild West: *a gold rush.* With the current economic uncertainty driving gold prices north of $1,800 an ounce, the town of Elko, Nev., is booming. Elko has had its ups and downs since its founding in the 1860s, but last year, Elko's mines produced more than $6 billion worth of the yellow stuff, making it the center of Nevada's mining production. How long the rush will last is anybody's guess. Meanwhile, newbies and old-timers fight over the scarcity of housing, temporarily occupying RV camps and showering at truck stops, while city fathers contemplate investments in Elko's infrastructure. It all depends on the price of gold.

Money is the most booby-trapped topic there is. Think how polarizing money is in the popular catch phrases of our culture. *Money makes the world go around. Money can't buy happiness (or love). Money is the root of all evil. Money changes everything.* I can only imagine how many hours on therapists' couches (at $200 an hour) are spent on this topic each year. And I'm not saying I have an easy answer here. How you think and feel about money is the by-product of a lifetime of conditioning. However, if you choose to Play Big, you'll need to deconstruct that conditioning and really examine how you're currently going for the gold—and ultimately what the "gold" should be.

I'd also offer a reality check for anyone lured by the mantra, "Do what you love and the money will come." In reality, not all jobs pay the same wage. And someone with a sincere passion to pursue a career as an orthopedic surgeon is likely to have a fatter bank account at the end of the day than one who, with equal drive and sincerity, chooses a career educating inner-city middle schoolers. But, as so many of my clients are proving, when you fully invest yourself in doing what you love, the value of that activity increases exponentially. What I'm talking about here is establishing a new paradigm for yourself where money is not the solitary litmus of success. In fact, the key for many people is to get focused on doing what they love and believe in 100%. What happens behind that strategy in terms of satisfaction and quality of life will completely transform your current ideas of compensation.

To begin the deconstruction process, I ask my clients to list some of the beliefs they have about money. Their lists vary, but usually include things like "I'd love to quit my job and do what I love, but I can't afford the pay cut" or "You have to suffer to be financially successful." In the second part of the exercise, I ask them to try and think of an example that refutes their belief—in other words, "Do you know someone who switched to doing what they really love and was able to go on paying their bills?" When they name an example, they begin to see that much of what they've believed about money is really a misconception—an attitude owing more to their conditioning than to actual fact.

I'd like to share three stories of people who overcame misconceptions about money and success to achieve a level of satisfaction in their lives they couldn't have previously imagined. Their accomplishments speak volumes on the power that focus and intention can wield and the rewards that can follow in their wake.

Remember the woman I told you about in the previous chapter, the one who switched from selling commercial real estate to brokering farm and ranch properties? She assumed that doing what she loved would cost her financially. She'd been very successful in commercial property sales, and feared that when she started Playing Big and doing what she really wanted, there would be a crippling dip in her income. Beneath that, we discovered she had a deeper misconception that also needed dismantling—that "If you love what you do, it's really not work." Or more basically, "People don't get paid to have *fun*—that's why they call it WORK!" It's not surprising, giving the Puritan work ethic most of us are weaned on, that we've forged this connection between money and discomfort. The more we earn, the more we must suffer, right? Together we saw how that axiom was playing out in her life—long, soul-crushing hours on the job in order to spend a few precious hours on weekends in her stable with the horses she loved.

The year she switched to brokering farm and ranch properties, her faith in Playing Big was certainly tested. Her income did drop as she experienced a pretty steep learning curve. For one thing, she started this new venture in the spring, when the farmers and ranchers she needed to reach were busy planting. However, she put her faith in building these relationships where she could, knowing that they were the foundation for her future success. Even though her purse was lighter, she chose to focus on adding value and being indispensable to her contacts, whether her efforts resulted in a sale or not. In lean times, she chose "How can I help?" over "How will I get paid?" as her mission statement.

Her initial reward wasn't in the form of money. Rather, she found herself compensated by the richness of the relationships she was building with people who, like herself, loved farm and ranch life. Her days were beginning to feel less like work, and—dare she say it—like *fun*? The more she focused on the *process* she was going through versus any *outcome*, the more everything began to flow.

Now for the happy ending. In the second year, her income from doing what she loves exceeded her best year in her old job. That said, my guess is that if you asked her what the best part of her new compensation package is, she'd probably say that she got her integrity back. She no longer has to masquerade in a business suit 60-plus hours a week only to catch a brief glimpse of her real love. She'd successfully traded up from a Lexus and high heels to an old truck and a comfortable pair of boots, and it had made all the difference.

The next story involves a guy who found his true purpose in the high-performance bike industry. Here's another money misconception: that you have to have a great big idea to be successful. At the outset, all he had was a few simple ideas and a passion to make high-performance bike dealers more successful. Immediately, the voices of dissent from those little Lilliputians in his head became deafening: "Who are you to start your own business?" or "Do you *really* know what you're doing here—and if you don't, *what if they find out?*"

So I encouraged him to put in earplugs and create his Playing Big business plan—a plan that focused first on the success of the bike dealers he was targeting. He began to see that his own genius was not found in some great galaxy-rocking idea, but in his uncanny ability to break his plan down into small pieces and working on each individual piece in a big way. In essence, his success came from the sum of the parts, and he was able to enhance the dealers' bottom lines and his own. Moral: small things often lead to big rewards—if you're willing to Play Big.

Here's the third story. Think you need lots of working capital and a stellar business reputation to be successful? Another misconception. This guy had neither. In fact, his success story begins at the bottom. He'd gone from flush to being in debt to the tune of six figures. His "take the money and run" approach had finally caught up with him. He owed half the people in town, and his reputation wasn't worth a cup of coffee.

For him, Playing Big was first about having a new vision for moving forward. Sensing that God loves "tryers" and that the universe smiles on people who are open, honest and direct, he decided to come clean. Bypassing bankruptcy as the easy exit, he walked door-to-door, promising everyone he owed that he would repay them in full. Whether they believed him or not didn't matter. What mattered was that he was now Playing Big, leading with honesty instead of his chin. It was tough, but it felt good. And it would get even better.

He also found his true purpose—in the area of urban real estate redevelopment. It turns out he had a heart for getting young professionals fresh out of college into their first apartment. He got creative, finding innovative ways to transform neglected old buildings into hip, affordable housing. His game plan for being 100% transparent in his dealings was paying off, both personally and professionally.

This happy ending was a while in the making. But at the end of 10 years, he had achieved a comfortable lifestyle and paid back everyone he owed at the beginning of this story. Imagine their surprise—and maybe his, too. His reputation in the field is so golden that when other urban redevelopers need answers, they call him. He has everything he lost and more. However, if asked, he'd reply that his greatest success is creating a fun, affordable place to live for so many young people on the first rung of their professional life.

These stories remind me that most of us perceive many limits on what we can do. We know the list by heart. But here's the kicker: most of those limits are set by us. Know how they train elephants? They start when they're babies by looping a chain around one ankle. The other end of the chain is fixed to a metal stake driven deep into the ground so the baby elephant can't get away. Over time, as the baby elephant grows, the chain is replaced with a rope; the metal stake is traded for a wooden stick. Ultimately, even the rope and stick are removed as unnecessary. By then the elephant is so accustomed to his tether that he doesn't stray, even when the actual restraint no longer exists. He's learned he cannot run, so he never tries.

Look carefully at your own beliefs about money. Have you unknowingly tethered yourself to misconceptions that aren't valid, that are keeping you from Playing Big? Then look down at your ankle. There's nothing there. It's time to run.

PLAYING BIGGER:

1. List three beliefs that you have about money. Are they true or just misconceptions? Think of examples that could prove these beliefs are misconceptions.

2. Research other stories on people who have gone from "riches" to "rags" and ended up doing a whole lot better than before.

3. Appraisal—Write out an appraisal of the things you value in your life. Your list should include things both material and nonmaterial. Assign an actual dollar value to everything on your appraisal list. Are there any surprises?

CHAPTER 4 – FOCUS

"That's been one of my mantras - focus and simplicity. Simple can be harder than complex. But it's worth it in the end because once you get there, you can move mountains."

Steve Jobs, founder of Apple Computer

ON APRIL 25, 1990, the Universe appeared to be opening up. NASA's space shuttle *Discovery* carried aloft the Hubble Telescope, a massive and revolutionary instrument that promised to deliver razor-sharp images of the heavens as we had never seen them before. Stars. Supernovas. Distant galaxies. The entire scientific community was buzzing with anticipation, but a few days after the Hubble went into orbit, it became clear that there was a problem—a big problem. The telescope's primary mirror, responsible for the clarity of those spectacular images that would transmit back to Earth, had been ground incorrectly. The shape of the mirror at its edges was too flat by only 2.2 microns—just over two-millionths of a meter. The result of this small manufacturing error was disastrous, and the images that came to Earth were fuzzy and out of focus. Scientists feared the worst: that they had a huge white elephant on their hands, at a launch cost of $1.5 billion.

So much of Playing Big depends on your focus. In the case of the Hubble, it took scientists and engineers three years and even more millions of dollars to fix the problem. I'm happy to tell you that if your vision of what you really want in life lacks clarity, you can fix it much faster than three years. This chapter will outline a simple process for focusing on what you want and, once your vision clears, on how to take hold of that vision in a manageable way that ensures you reach your goal.

First, let's understand why lack of focus is so debilitating. It's a simple law of physics: when we focus our energies on too many things, our energy is dissipated. The life force that drives us to chase dreams and conquer mountains can become fragmented and diluted by the sheer number of directions in which we're moving. We can find ourselves, at the end of the day, year or 10 years, exhausted and feeling like we have little to show for all our efforts.

The analogy of digging a lot of shallow holes versus going deep toward your real desire seems apt here. It's true that the shallow holes imply a lot of activity, and you'll begin to see this if you're currently surrounded by them and have always prided yourself in being busy. Here's the problem: the multiplicity of your efforts has prevented you from accomplishing anything that, in your heart, really matters. In other words, it's a lot of digging for never having struck oil. It's precisely at this point of realization that many of my clients have come to me. It's usually with some sadness as they recognize that all their efforts, all those shallow holes won't, at the end of their lives, really matter.

Here's a simple exercise I use with my clients to get them focused. Make a list of all the things you're passionate about—those special things that give you such a powerful charge and sense of self-worth and accomplishment that you'd do them for free if you could. A sample list is seen below:

—Learn Mandarin Chinese
—Get in great physical shape
—Grow an organic garden
—Get my MBA
—Teach a class in martial arts
—Open a homeless shelter
—Travel to Australia
—Learn to play the guitar
—Write a screenplay
—Build a vacation home

This is your initial list. Make it as exhaustive as possible, even including things you may just now realize you are passionate about, thoughts or dreams that have never showed up on paper until this moment.

Now you have your Playing Big list, and it's time to focus. You do that by process of elimination. Take your big list and cut it in half. If you have 20 things on your big list, cut it down to 10. Then cut it again to three things and rank those three in order of importance to you. Throughout this focusing exercise you should continue to ask yourself, "What here is essential for me in order to feel alive?" It's important that what you end up with has a significant payoff for you personally. It's this "prize" that will sustain you through the process of achieving it. Without it, you're more than likely to lose heart along the way.

This focusing exercise helped my first and most important client: me. Like a lot of people I now work with, I had been a consummate doer. I started my own ad agency, which grew up to serve a number of regional and national clients. Along the way, my wife and I raised four kids—no small task. And I gave back, donating hours of work to create public service advertising for worthy causes. I was president of our local Boys & Girls Club board. My days and my calendar were chock-full of meetings and tasks, and I was proud that I could be so damn busy.

All that time, it was slowly creeping from the back of my mind to the front that I was really frustrated. I had been so busy *doing* that I'd never stopped long enough to ask myself those fundamental questions. Was I having any *fun*? Did any of this frenzied activity really matter? Would I be able to take my last breath knowing I'd found my true purpose? I had distracted myself with insignificant activity that fueled my ego and soothed my self-centered fear. I knew I could shift my life into a higher gear if only I could find the lever and then muster the courage to pull it.

The ensuing days were among the darkest I have ever known. But I offer this to you as a profound word of hope. If I had not gotten to that low point—gazing upon my own vast landscape of shallow holes—I would never have reclaimed my true purpose to live the life I live today. As hard as it was, I had to get *there* to get *here*.

Enter Kevin Ross, my first coach. An email from Kevin appeared in my mailbox around this time. He was soliciting new clients, and his email asked if I was stuck and wanting to get to the next level. As a seasoned ad man, I'm generally pretty immune to marketing ploys, but Kevin's really resonated with me. He had put his finger on exactly where I found myself at that time.

And I bit. I called his office one evening after normal business hours and happened to catch him in. He described how things worked—that I was to pay him a huge fee up-front. I swallowed pretty hard when I heard the price tag. It seemed then (and now) to be a lot of money. But I understood later the logic of his approach. Kevin wasn't interested in dabblers. He knew that for our relationship to succeed, I had to be all in. The fear factor, plus the gravitational pull of "stability," could only be overcome if I was completely invested. I got out my checkbook and scuttled my lifeboats.

Like yours, my first assignment was to create a list of things I was passionate about, things that were so personally rewarding and motivating that I'd be happy to do them and skip the paycheck. One of Kevin's mantras was that if I got crystal clear about "what" I really want to do, the "how" would appear. I wrote pages and pages about my passions—he'd send them back to me for more clarification. It felt unnerving, but again there was method in this apparent madness. His challenges served to fortify me, giving me the assurance that I wasn't just *saying* this is what I really wanted—but that *I really wanted it*! He needed to make sure I was locked in a laser-like focus, with a clear sense of purpose that would guide me to fulfillment. This exercise also had the effect of stoking my internal boiler to the task, so that by the time he finally said "Go!" I felt I could overcome any obstacle in pursuit of my goal.

I had narrowed my list, and by process of elimination got down to my two top picks:

1. Create a program to help U.S. service members returning from active duty who were suffering from post-traumatic stress disorder (PTSD).
2. Build an executive performance consulting and coaching business complete with a website, marketing materials and a system for launching and developing the business.

I was beginning to understand the importance of clarity. The more exciting the word-picture I painted of my vision, the more it compelled me to see that vision through to fruition. I knew I had to state my vision in a way that got my blood going, in words that would make me want to jump out of bed each day instead of hitting the snooze button and rolling over for another 10 minutes.

I finally knew what I wanted and had put it down on paper. A significant accomplishment, right? Now what? Because fundamentally, the move from thinking big to Playing Big involves taking action. Now that you have your vision, how do you scale that Everest and have fun while you're doing it? One of the inherent challenges you'll face is true of any race: the first and last five minutes of the 10K are incredibly exciting, but those Ks in the middle of the marathon can really pull you down if you don't have an effective strategy before you begin.

My first piece of strategic advice involves breaking your vision down into manageable chunks. Mind that old adage about not biting off more than you can chew. Having a sense of accomplishment along the way will motivate you to keep going, so divide your tasks accordingly.

As I began to breakdown my vision for serving military families, a course of action emerged that involved fundraising, making strategic alliances with mental health care leaders and raising public awareness of the affects of PTSD on U.S. service members and their families. My enthusiasm and motivation grew as I continued to ask myself key questions like, "If in 90 days I could raise $50,000 to help military families, would it make a difference in how I feel about myself and how I am engaged in spending my time?"

A second important piece of your strategy involves accountability—a topic I touched on in an earlier chapter but want to discuss now in more detail. I can tell you from my own experience that having someone to whom you'll be fully accountable is essential to achieving your vision. In my case, my accountability partner was the professional coach I was working with at the time my life came into focus. The first thing this coach made me agree to was that I would be completely committed to achieving my vision for the next 90 days. I gave him the right to hold me fully accountable for actually doing what I said I was going to do. To have a successful relationship with your accountability partner, you must have complete transparency. So I committed to do "whatever it takes" and gave him the right to hold me to that standard.

I also found that the value of this kind of third-party support went far beyond having a cop who made sure I followed through on my action plan. In the larger sense, my coach helped me *keep* my focus. As I said before, the beginning and the end of any race is exciting. But Kevin was able to help lift up my vision through those difficult middle Ks, kept me from giving up during those long days of striving toward a goal that seemed impossibly far off in the distance. His role was not only practical, it was spiritual. He encouraged me to remain fully engaged in the pursuit of my vision and helped me celebrate as each little brick got set into what

I was building. And every now and then, he'd remind me who I am and why I'm doing this.

I've used my own experience here for two reasons. First, to show you that I eat my own cooking, and second, to demonstrate that if you're focused and follow the steps I've outlined here, you can accomplish extraordinary things in only 90 days. I got the coaching business up and running, complete with a website and all the marketing materials I needed to attract and serve clients. The At Ease program (visit **www.atease.org** for more information), now in its third year of helping service members and families, is functioning through a major regional social service agency and provides complete assessment and treatment for veterans suffering from PTSD. To date, we've raised more than $1 million to fuel the program. And in February of this year, At Ease will begin clinical trials of a new cutting-edge treatment program for PTSD—the first research of it's kind in the U.S.

As proud as I am of these accomplishments, the real prize was what I discovered about myself in the process. That it was possible to regain your vision. That by getting focused and using every bit of elbow grease toward what I really wanted, I could create the kind of life for myself that I'd always imagined. A life where I finally—*finally*—felt fulfilled. I'm not telling you all this because I'm extraordinary; on the contrary, it is the power of intense focus that is extraordinary.

As I look at my experience, I see clearly how easily we get trapped in the minutia of life. You may recognize the metaphoric question about how you get rocks, sand and gravel into a vase. We're challenged by the fact that this stuff varies in size, from large stones (what's most important to us) to gravel (things of lesser importance) to sand (the least important). The urgency of the least important distract us from the really important. Then, too late, we realize that our vase is already full, and we've left no room for the big stones—the things that in the end matter most to us.

Playing Big is about using the opposite approach. If you start filling your life with the big stones—the things that you've realized are most important, the minutia will flow around them. But most importantly, in the final analysis, you'll have the satisfaction of knowing that nothing you really value was left on the table.

Again, I feel compelled to make the distinction between *simple* and *easy*. Looking back, there wasn't much about achieving either of my visions that I'd call easy. However, the simplicity of having narrowed down what I really wanted to an extremely short list, then breaking down the tasks to achieve them, created a model of action that ensured every ounce of effort would pay off. No more shallow holes!

I'm hopeful by now you're already making a mental list of what you'd love to do. Begin to put it on paper. As you list, continue to ask yourself, "When have I felt the most *alive*? When have I made the biggest contribution to others lives?" It could well be the most important thing you've ever done.

Three years after its launch, the mirror problems were fixed, and in 1993, the Hubble telescope began transmitting photos of unspeakable beauty back to Earth. Stars being born. Spiral galaxies interacting. Strings of cosmic pearls. Focus your imagination. The possibilities are infinite.

PLAYING BIGGER:

1. Write a journal entry about a time in your life when you felt incredibly satisfied. What were you engaged in? Recall how you felt at that time. What made it special, lifting you above your normal routine? What did you bring to others' lives?

2. Name three people who, based on your observation, are achieving a high degree of fulfillment in their lives. What do you observe about how they operate in life that gives them a superior level of satisfaction?

3. Flow—Defining your true purpose involves paying attention to when you're in a state of flow—when the task you're doing seems effortless and time evaporates. Pay attention for the next week and record how you feel when you're in this flow state, and what you're occupied with that seems to generate this state. What happens to you? What happens to others?

CHAPTER 5 – GETTING REAL

"Then you will know the truth, and the truth will set you free."
from the Gospel of John

FRANK WILLIAM ABAGNALE. Recognize the name? If you don't, you will in a minute. He's now a high-level security consultant. But in the 1960s, he was one of the world's most successful con artists—a confidence man, check forger and escape artist par excellence. At the height of his career, Abagnale had floated more than $2.5 million worth of exquisitely forged checks in 26 countries around the globe. He was a brilliant imposter, able to impersonate an airline pilot, a medical doctor, an attorney and even a U.S. Bureau of Prisons agent. On the lam, he once escaped from a taxiing jetliner. Frank's real-life adventures formed the basis for the movie *Catch Me if You Can* starring Leonardo DiCaprio. His story also inspired the Tony Award-winning Broadway musical of the same title.

Now that you know Frank Abagnale, I'd like you to meet another con man who may be a little closer to your heart: you. No, I'm not suggesting that you're out there writing phony checks or shinnying down a plane's landing gear to elude the authorities. The con I'm talking about is not telling yourself the truth. The lie that millions tell themselves daily—that they love the job they really hate, that if they just hang in there and apply themselves things will get better, that each drop of sanguine suffering inches them a little closer to the Great American Dream and their ultimate satisfaction.

It's worth wondering why it's just so damn hard to be honest with ourselves. If our birthright is to live in our true purpose, to Play Big in all things and not count the cost, then why do we settle? What choke chain holds us, catches us at the throat whenever instinct pulls us toward our deepest desire? First, if you identify with this plight, you are not alone. Most of my clients must come to this baseline realization—that they're not being straight with themselves—before we can move forward. I'd also offer that not all of my clients are miserable in their current work. Some realize that they could find fulfillment right where they are if only they could find a way to Play Bigger—a way to leave their fears behind and switch from a black-and-white version of themselves to something in full and vibrant color.

To be sure, the truth is not always easy to deal with, particularly if fear of the truth has held you back for a good chunk of your adult life. But let's see if we can debunk a few of what I've seen are the primary fear cons, the leg irons that hobble many who have then gone on to bigger things once they break those shackles.

Here's the first fear con: that truth is the harbinger of Armageddon. It usually goes something like this: if I pursue what I really love, I'll never earn enough to make ends meet and will end my days in complete and utter destitution. I'll lose the support of my loved ones and friends. If I let my soul drive in the direction of my dreams and aspirations, the sky will fall, Mother Earth will open up to swallow me whole, letting out a lusty belch as my lone epitaph. If the melodrama in reading this has caused you to smile, it's only because I've exposed this fear to the light of day. Viewed in full sunlight, it's easy to label it laughable. But until you recognize this fear for what it really is, it will keep you anchored in place. Every year, the weight of this ball-and-chain will double.

The second fear con contains an interesting paradox: that if I get real about who I am and what I really want, people will think I'm a phony. In other words, if I begin to act on what's true to me, it will feel completely false, both to me and to those around me. As gently as I can, I'm here to tell you that if you're not being truthful with yourself now, it's more than likely those around you know it already. Again, you're not alone. Many clients come to me earnestly desiring to be real, to drop the pretense, to stop being the imposter they've come to loathe and just be themselves. That transition—from the person you're impersonating to the real you—is often painful. You'll soon discover that whatever pain accompanies this transition is nothing compared to the daily discomfort you experience while afraid to be who you really are.

I've left the biggest fear con for last, because it goes deeper than the previous two. For some, the biggest fear is "I sense that I have the goods to Play Big, but fear I'll never be able to summon up the nerve, the chutzpah, the courage to crack out of this chrysalis so my true self can emerge." And here's the kicker that goes right to your solar plexus, "… and if I should try this and I fail, it's proof positive that I'm somehow deficient and should never have tried in the first place." I find this myth that we're deficient at some fundamental level is quite prevalent. Our culture has become a cult of self-improvement, teaching us to doubt our innate abilities. We think of ourselves as a fixer-upper home that could be flipped for a decent profit if only we could finally get everything fixed. If I assure you of nothing else in this book, let it be that, at a fundamental level, you are supremely capable. When you acknowledge what's true for you and begin to act upon that truth, the real you will emerge. Playing Big is not about pretending to be someone or something you're not. It's about finally being who you *really* are—that person Nature has predestined to be big—and, having discovered that ability, will never return to your smaller past.

I'm reminded of the story of another one of my clients. He was in his mid-forties and had been successful in two other careers, but since the time he was nine years old, he dreamed of a life on the stage. For years, his successes in these other careers had effectively masked his frustration that he wasn't living up to who he really was. He'd faithfully worn the costume and spoken in the dialect of a businessman, but in this role he was growing less and less convincing. Finally, he had to admit—to himself and those he cared about—that he had to follow his heart. There was a bigger spotlight out there, and he was going to find it.

A full year before he hung up his corporate hat to chase this dream, his Lilliputians mounted a full-scale attack. They flung doubts at him like a hail of boulders launched from medieval catapults. He couldn't sleep. He lost 15 pounds. The cold grip of fear did its level best to convince him, even before he'd begun, that he was about to make the worst mistake of his life. What would his business partners say? What if he ran out of money? What if he eviscerated his former life only to arrive in New York and discover, in short order, that he had no talent? And finally, what would it be like to descend on all fours and crawl back home in defeat to a chorus of "I told you so"—the loudest and most strident being his own?

Once he made the leap, things got better. He began to glimpse the power in being who he really was. His first year in New York took everything he had and then some. But today, more than four years into his odyssey, he has experienced success he could never have imagined. He just finished his third tour to Spain with one of New York's finest gospel ensembles. And he just got the lead role in an independent film that will be shooting this spring. I don't need to ask him if it was really worth everything—the fear, the doubts, the digestive problems he had to go through to get there. His beaming face holds the answer.

This fear mongering we put ourselves through reminds me of another myth, courtesy of the ancient Greeks. Pandora, the first woman in Greek mythology, was given a jar by Zeus that was said to contain all the evils of the world. She was cautioned never to unseal the jar, because if she did, those evils would be unleashed on mankind for eternity. When you're not being straight with yourself about who you really are and what you want, your true self may feel like that jar you're afraid to unleash upon the world. My goal is to move you beyond the myth. Client after client has discovered that when they let go and are truly themselves, all their fear of Armageddon dissipates like smoke in a good breeze.

That was pretty much how it happened for me. When I was ready to stop pretending and start being who I really am, those fears chased me like some hornets whose nest had been upset. Ironically, I was in fact saner than I had ever been, and this newfound sense of sanity steadied me in a way I could not have predicted. I had finally gotten my priorities straight, finally admitted that what was more important to me than anything was to be about the business of helping people and making a difference. And the difference in me was evident.

Finally, I want to tell you a story about one of my clients that demonstrates the power of being who you really are. "Mary" works for a large corporation, and is responsible for maintaining a strong relationship with one of this corporation's most important—and difficult—clients. Being fairly new to the company, Mary first sought counsel from her superiors on solving the problem. They could offer little advice, and mostly reminded her how much revenue that client brought in—and not to screw it up.

Fortunately, Mary was not the long-suffering type. She knew who she was—and also who she was not. The corporate culture would have urged her to don her oilskins, hunker down and do her best to weather the hurricane that came her way on a daily basis. However, she knew what was true for her, and she ventured to a place where no one before her had the courage to go. Mary invited her nemesis to dinner, and over several bottles of wine, she told her the truth. "This relationship really isn't working," she told her nemesis kindly but candidly, "and my guess is that it's not working for you, either. Can we talk about how to fix it?"

I'm sure you could have heard a pin drop at that restaurant table. Her client was completely disarmed by Mary's candor. She confessed that she was frustrated too, that she felt lost and out of place—and was deathly afraid of "screwing up" herself. The confessional my client created then became a crucible for the solution. By the time the last drop of wine had been drunk and the check paid, the two women had come to an understanding and hammered out a way to move forward.

I often use her story when I work with management teams on leadership development. Like everything else, there are myths about leadership, and particularly how leaders are made, but as this example illustrates, leadership is not about tactics. There is no set of tips or tricks that make a leader. There is no manual in a three-ring binder. This woman became a leader when she recognized who she was—that she wasn't someone who wanted to spend the next five years being somebody's doormat—and she had the courage to act upon that truth. Not surprisingly, when she reported the results to her superiors, they were dumbfounded. "You did WHAT?" they asked. They feared the Pandora effect—that telling the truth meant losing business, jobs and revenue. The world would come unraveled. Instead, she proved that being who you are is not only healthy, it's good business.

By choosing to Play Big, by overriding her own fears and those of her superiors, Mary saved a client relationship that was literally worth millions to her corporation. And by simply *telling the truth*, she demonstrated a skill that's so rare in corporate America today it's practically nonexistent. I'm proud to say that she's also now engendering this in the people she supervises in that company. Her ability to say the simple truth, to respect and trust that people can handle the truth is already becoming her legacy. By showing the benefits of Playing Big, she's empowering others to Play Big, too.

I hope her story encourages you. You may now be at that critical point—tired of pretending to be someone else, and longing to be who you really are. Remember Frank Abagnale. He started out as a con man, and ended up on the right side of the law. If you're conning yourself, there's a simple solution. Start telling the truth. And watch what happens. You're starting to Play Big ... and this is only the beginning.

PLAYING BIGGER:

1. Fear Factor—Imagine yourself Playing Big, in a new job, living in a different part of the country or even another country, whatever you dream to do. As you imagine, notice what fears pop up. Write them down, and examine them one by one. Which ones are real? Which ones lose power over you as you scrutinize them?

2. Fearless Players—Make a list of people you've known whom you consider fearless. Spend some time with one of them if you can. Ask them about their attitudes toward life's fears and what they've learned that helps them Play Big.

CHAPTER 6 – LEADING BIG

"If your actions inspire others to dream more, learn more,
do more and become more, you are a leader."
John Quincy Adams

THOUGH NOT AS FAMOUS as his father, John Quincy Adams was nevertheless a remarkable man. The precise details of his leadership style have faded into antiquity, but you can surmise his management skill when you look at the span of his accomplishments. Many historians believe that Adams was the greatest diplomat and Secretary of State this country has ever known. He negotiated the treaty that ended the War of 1812, wrote the Monroe Doctrine and was a leading opponent of slavery long before Lincoln brought forth his Emancipation Proclamation. As our sixth President, John Quincy Adams is credited with modernizing the American economy in a turbulent age, when new ways of communication were revolutionizing the workings of U.S. trade and commerce. Thanks largely to Adams' skill and foresight, goods, money and people began travelling faster and more efficiently than ever before. He accomplished all this despite a lifelong battle with depression and more than a few "to-the-moon" expectations of his parents, John and Abigail.

What Adams clearly learned—and what I teach—is that leadership cannot be shrink-wrapped. If you've been under the impression that great leaders are made of a smart set of tips and tactics, prepare to explore an alternate universe.

As I've worked with new managers of major corporations on leadership development, I've come to understand why this idea is so prevalent. It's an attractive notion—that everything needed to create outstanding leaders might be condensed to fill a standard three-ring binder. A perfectly consistent plan that can be adopted by the entire company. A set of answers to all known questions that ensures decisive leadership and guarantees return on investment. What could possibly be wrong with that? My answer: everything.

The truth is that we're not led by tips and tactics. We're ultimately led by people. True leaders inspire others to greatness because they have first found that greatness within themselves.

It's easiest to pinpoint what I'm talking about if you stop for a minute and recall some of the qualities of leaders who have really inspired you—and I hope there have been a few. I often use this question as a point of departure when initiating work with leadership teams. Not surprisingly, their responses are fairly consistent, and include things like consistency, a positive attitude, authenticity and transparency, humility and the ability to empower.

That empowering or coach-like quality makes me immediately think of my good friend, mentor and former advertising client Jack Baker. I worked with Jack when he was running the chain of supermarkets his father started, which still bears the family name. At the time, we were a tiny ad agency pitching a very big account. Somehow, Jack had the faith to hire us. I know now that he picked us largely because he saw something that maybe we hadn't yet seen in ourselves—that he fully expected us to play full out—*to Play Big*. And not just that—that we could do it exceptionally. In that empowerment lies the magic of leadership. What Jack discovered, as many other real leaders have, was that when you give people credit over and above what they may even give themselves, almost always they will up their game and fill the gap.

And we did. When I showed up during Thanksgiving or over the Fourth of July to help sack groceries at a Baker's store, it wasn't just because I was trying to be a good vendor. It was because Jack inspired me to bring the best of myself I could possibly bring. I knew that what I was doing was important to him, and I wanted to be part of it.

If all this is sounding a bit warm and fuzzy, don't be deceived. There's a good reason for it that goes right to the bottom line. Make no mistake: the competitive landscape grows ever flatter. Advances in technology and the free flow of information have made an environment where any firm's competitive advantage is measured in smaller and smaller increments. What remains to set you apart is the degree to which your team is invested in what they do. This is the undiscovered country, and it lies solely within the hearts and minds of those you lead. A win here can virtually redefine your advantage and reposition you for success—not in numbers of retail outlets or supply-chain logistics, but in how passionate people are about creating something exceptional, whatever your widget happens to be.

This awakening of the national workforce has never been more crucial, especially among Generations X and Y. Recent studies have shown that the level of engagement of these folks in their current jobs is at a historic low. What's needed—and needed right now—is leadership. We need leaders who know how to unlock the potential of everyone in their charge, leaders who can turn the current disengagement in the workforce from being a drain on the firm and our economy into the boom that creates the next iPad, the next revolution.

Earlier I referred to this as the undiscovered country. The most powerful and exciting force available to companies today lies within their employees. If you're a leader, it's up to you to tap that force. To succeed, you first have to be 100% engaged yourself. If you're not genuinely excited, you'll find yourself driving an empty bandwagon. The values that workers most prize in those who lead (passion, compassion and authenticity), have to be real. Leadership cannot be faked.

Now let's move from theory into practice. If you're following my argument, and you're a leader with a sincere desire to unlock the true potential of your workers, you may well ask, "How?" Again, I caution you that true leadership isn't about a series of tips and tactics—and I will offer you none here. It's about showing up each day on the job as passionately as possible and living up to the values—passion, compassion, authenticity—that more than likely inspired you to give your best performance. I speak of values because it's been my experience working with business leaders across a wide spectrum of companies that most of them are accustomed to leading from a set of objectives, not values. So acknowledge that this approach is a departure from the norm. It's not that these leaders don't have values. Rather, these values that could completely transform the workplace have simply been undervalued, pushed further and further into the background as the daily pressure to eek out bigger objectives with a smaller and less-invested work force has grown more arduous.

Here's the best place to start: name a leader that has inspired you. Someone whose values on the job helped you excel, who saw that undiscovered potential within you and collaborated with you to bring it out. If several leaders come to mind, choose the one that has the most power for you.

We're now going to construct a variation on the Big Wheel I presented in Chapter One. This is your Leading Big Wheel. Think of the values this leader you identified in the previous paragraph brought to the table. Try to list eight of them and write them as the eight segments of your wheel. Focus on those values you want to exhibit yourself that also inspired you. If it worked for you, it will work for those you're about to lead.

Okay, you're now looking at your Leading Big Wheel. It's divided into eight pie pieces, each piece labeled with a leadership value you admire and aspire to. Now evaluate your performance against each of the values you've selected. If you labeled one of your segments EMPOWERMENT, give yourself a score from 1 to 10. That is your honest assessment of how you're delivering on that value today.

Here's an example of how powerful this little exercise is in practice. Recently I worked with a woman who had been promoted to a leadership position in her Fortune 500 firm. She had no trouble coming up with a leader she admired—a woman who was her boss in that same firm several years ago.

Something significant happened as she looked at her Leading Big Wheel and the values she had written in the various segments. As she graded herself from 1 to 10 on those values, she saw that there were substantial gaps between the boss she admired and her own performance in the six months since she'd taken on this leadership role. Her candid evaluation of her own performance made her realize that what she was doing was not the model of leadership she wanted to create. What she wanted was a model that worked—her former boss's model. She knew that if she wanted to get the results out of her team that this boss had extracted from her, she would have to change.

So we took a closer look at her Leading Big Wheel. One of the values she put a high priority on was EMPOWERMENT—the quality that encourages people to find their own way, invent their own solutions and color outside the lines. To clarify, this isn't the "Give 'em enough rope to hang themselves" ploy that is sometimes practiced in corporate America. If it's true empowerment, it's more like "Give 'em enough rope in hopes that they'll tie the golden lasso." She prized empowerment values above all others because she knew what it had done for her, and for its potential to ignite the team she was now leading.

However, when she scored her own performance, she saw that when it came to empowerment, she was only delivering a "4" out of a possible "10." She also knew why. She admitted that she was a micromanager, a henpecker and a real hoverer. I loved the candor with which she said, "Honestly, if I were working for me right now, I wouldn't be pulling with everything I've got, either."

We both knew we were in a great spot—there was nowhere to go but up. So I asked her, "What would be an acceptable score for you in EMPOWERMENT?" Her answer: an 8 or 9. Here she began to see another benefit of this exercise—it helped her get her priorities straight. It may not be necessary to perform at a "10" on every value you've listed. But, if the one you've identified as the most important—the one that gets your own blood pumping—is the very thing you're not delivering on, you must re-focus on what's essential.

The question becomes, "How do I empower my team at an "8" or "9" level versus the current "4"? The answer was easier than she might have thought. Again, I asked her to recall the interactions she'd had with her memorable boss. "When she empowered you, how did she go about it—to get you to be all in?" My client recalled that early in their relationship, her former boss made it clear that all she wanted was exceptional work. She identified the "what," and left the "how" up to my client. In other words, "I expect nothing but the best from you, but I'll let you determine how to give that to me—and by the way, I still need it on Friday." It was indeed challenging, my client recalled. The expectations were clearly set. Again, she recalled that being given the latitude to create her own path was transformative. Empowered by her boss, she set out to tie the golden lasso.

I can tell you that today this woman is on her way to being an exceptional leader because of this simple exercise. She saw what she was doing wrong. She knew that a higher level of empowerment was important and necessary both to her and her team. And she came up with a plan that included specific steps that made her more empowering, including getting regular feedback from her troops on how much of that golden rope they believed she was letting out.

Like most things in the Playing Big arena, I encourage leaders to think in terms of their first 90 days at the helm. I've already shown by example in previous chapters that you can do great things in a small amount of time if you really get focused. In the case of the client I just mentioned, what she accomplished in just three months, behind a focused plan to empower her team, surprised even her.

Consistency is also a key value—one that may have shown up on your own Leading Big Circle, and I'd like to briefly address it here. There's an old quip that the two most opportune times for a leader are during the first 90 days—and then every minute thereafter. You may evaluate your team members' performances annually, but they evaluate your performance every minute of the workday. We all know that talk is cheap. However, when you show up consistently and really do what you say you're going to do, your team will fall in line. Like a good parent, if you model the right behavior, others will follow.

There's another important value real leaders engender that demonstrates Playing Big: they are willing to stretch and take risks. You'll find it difficult to get your team to Play Big if you're unwilling to do the same. Last month, I worked with a group of mid-level managers in a large firm. Their assignment was to bring me three ideas of things they could accomplish by the end of the year—things so momentous that to get them done would signify a big win for them, their team and the entire company. The ideas they brought back were disappointing but also predictable; most were simply things that their superiors had already told them to do.

I could see their point of view, and certainly businesses from now until the end of time will have objectives, initiatives and quotas that must be met. I assured my participants that I understood this. Then I asked, "Okay, say you were able to accomplish this stuff you listed. On an exhilaration scale from 1 to 10, how would having done that make you feel?" My point: if there's nothing on those lists that gets their palms a little sweaty or would truly make them feel fulfilled, then all they're doing is sentencing themselves to one more year skinning their noses on the corporate grindstone. Moving beyond their evident chagrin, I asked, "What else is possible? If the budget and time were all unlimited, what could you come up with? What could you do that's really exhilarating, and maybe even a little scary?" I asked this not to discount their previous list (which amounted to those things that are minimally acceptable in order to keep their jobs), but to pry open the door to wider possibilities. "What could you do that would make a headline—in your company newsletter or elsewhere? What magnificent act would win you and your team firm-wide recognition?" My intent was to get them to go beyond what is sadly an increasingly common aspiration these days—to just make it safely through another year and not get fired.

There's a real need to do this, to broaden your focus and imagine that your possibilities are unlimited. You do it for the business. You do it to make a profit. But there's an even grander purpose. You do it to grow massively. *Your* growth. The growth of those who call you "boss." How will you know when you get there? In Lao Tzu's words, "The best of leaders know when the job is done, when the task is accomplished, the people will say we have done it ourselves."

PLAYING BIGGER:

1. Leadership Traits—Describe your leadership style in a series of adjectives, e.g. "decisive," "inspiring," etc. This can be aspirational as well. You can list traits you don't feel you have, but wish you did, to round out your leadership style. Then follow the exercise I described earlier in the chapter with the Leading Big Wheel.

2. Leader Challenges—Recall a time when you encountered a significant challenge as a leader. How might you have done things differently to achieve a more positive outcome? And if the outcome was positive, what did you learn about yourself or the situation that will help you in similar situations?

CHAPTER 7 – PLAYING BIG IN A SMALL CULTURE

"I am big. It's the pictures that got small."

Norma Desmond in *Sunset Boulevard*

SHE WAS OFF HER ROCKER. Norma Desmond, an iconic, though fading, silent film star in Billy Wilder's 1950 classic, utters these words to the screenwriter who she hopes will help engineer her comeback. As wacky as Norma sounds, she was trying to deal with what millions are struggling with today—searching for a way to Play Big in a world that, by all appearances, has turned decidedly small.

This was evident in a recent coaching session I conducted. First, I asked a client to keep track of his day, noting how many minutes he spent in each of his daily activities. I then asked him to list his top four values—the things that meant most to him—and cross-reference the two. How much of his time on a daily basis did he spend exhibiting his core values? Almost without exception, he discovered that he spent very little of his day displaying the values he had identified as most important. His desire to Play Big, as stated in his core values, was largely just talk.

This exercise dramatizes a disconnect which I believe is all too common today: people think that the values they hold and the work they do must be almost mutually exclusive. With the national unemployment rate nearing 8% (2012), we've adopted a Depression Era mind-set. We find ourselves parroting the same things they were saying back in the 1930s—in tough times, cling
to the status quo. If ever there was a time to avoid rocking the boat, it is now.

At a panel discussion I conducted this year with business leaders, I challenged the participants to dismantle this ideology. The first of many participants expressed the fear that the only way to live their values at work was to work elsewhere.

"Are you saying we should just stop going to work?" one participant asked. Another chimed in, "So what if I quit work? I can't *afford* that. I have obligations, I have a family to take care of, etc. …" Here again we're seeing the rise of the Lilliputians, those little limiting beliefs that, when left unexamined, can loom larger than life itself. Without scrutiny, these Lilliputians have an easy time immobilizing us under the tyrannical conclusion (really theirs, not ours) that because of this economy, no sane man or woman would do ANYTHING that might inch them one hour closer to getting fired.

Another limiting belief the Lilliputians promote is that if you are actually willing to reach for a higher goal, this reaching is a surefire route to your termination. To stretch beyond the accepted boundaries of creativity, innovation or ambition would, by definition, earn you your pink slip.

My role in these discussions is to help people realize the perception/reality disconnect here. For example, if I brought my employer a creative idea, how could that be *bad*? Isn't there at least a possibility that it might be appreciated? At the very least, isn't it likely that it would do no harm? Admittedly, there are corporate cultures I've encountered that are so toxic, the only hope for survival is to bury yourself in your own foxhole—a sort of living interment. But in most cases, simply asking yourself, "Is this true?" can begin to make those Lilliputians run for cover. However, as long as our fear of getting fired remains unexamined, it remains our automatic response.

Realistically, in today's economic climate, for both individuals and businesses, *there is nothing riskier than playing it safe*. In fact, playing it safe is not a success strategy at all. It's a race to the bottom. Imagine a pro football game if both teams played nothing but defense. A lot of blocking and tackling. Taping up ankles with the cheapest tape—or not at all. Using up every conceivable time-out. But no passing. No running the ball. No touchdowns. Who would watch? And yet, that's essentially what you get when a company exclusively plays defense and makes its entire operating scheme about smallness, doing what's safe and continually cutting costs. The climate right now finds many companies thus engaged: gun-shy on investing in R&D, holding off on hiring and dialing down operating costs to new levels of severity.

History has shown that the rewards for playing small are equally small. Companies like Apple that maintain a Playing Big mantra have shown that they can thrive even in tough economic times. TIME magazine reported in February 2012 that Apple's value is now greater than that of Microsoft and Google combined. I'm certain that the quickest way to have gotten fired by Steve Jobs was to play small. Apple's core values and the notion of playing small are simply antithetical.

Apple wasn't afraid to Play Big by marketing the Newton more than 20 years ahead of its time. Had it not taken that risk back in 1987, we might not have the iPad today. Whatever Apple lost on the Newton has been recouped exponentially in iPad sales, which continue to increase year after year. Apple now sits on an estimated $100 billion in cash. Compare this to companies stuck in survival mode. Again, it's a prodigious race to the bottom.

I witness this unwitting race for last place among companies who, by playing small, have reduced their entire industry to a mere commodity. That is, they have no market differentiator left other than price. Companies who live by cutting cost will also die by it. If your only strategy is cost control, you'll most certainly get what you pay for: the minimum—flat revenues, underperforming employees and increasing vulnerability to competitors who aren't afraid to take risks.

This is an issue of national and even global significance, one that could eventually threaten our sovereignty among nations if it remains unchecked. If the U.S., whose economy was built on a freewheeling and entrepreneurial business culture, continues to pull in its horns, we will be increasingly outpaced by our less conservative neighbors in the world marketplace.

A special challenge exists today for publicly traded companies who are accountable to shareholders every 90 days. How do these companies manage shareholders' long-term expectations during extended periods of innovation, when they're building future value but are not likely to see a short-term uptick in the share price? Little wonder that many of the most innovative companies remain in private hands as long as they can, or at a minimum, have elected not to provide quarterly guidance (e.g. Berkshire Hathaway).

I hope I've at least begun to dispel the myth that the road back to a booming U.S. economy is paved with cost cutting and adopting a wait-and-see approach. The real road back is to start Playing Bigger—today. Otherwise, we'll just get more of the same. At a minimum, if we fail to recognize opportunity, we certainly should understand risk. The riskiest thing we can do—for ourselves, our corporations and even our world—is to continue playing small.

THE EMPEROR'S SMALL CLOTHES—I'd like to share with you this lesson from my own coaching experience that powerfully illustrates how playing small forces both individuals and corporations to pay a big price. A mid-level IT manager I'm working with received a mandate from his superior to acquire a new technology for the company. It was a major investment that would cost the company millions. Somewhere in the course of implementing this technology, my client discovered several serious flaws. The new technology was, in fact, the wrong solution and would not function as expected or hoped. Among all the possible solutions, it was far and away the most expensive. Because it was the wrong solution, it would require even more investment in costly add-ons—additional software and consultant fees—to make the system function at even a barely acceptable level.

This mid-level IT guy clearly saw that the emperor had no clothes. What did he do? Well, let's look at his options. Option one was to speak up. Announce to the corporate fathers (including his boss—and remember, this was his boss's idea) that what they had undertaken was a huge, expensive mistake. As the messenger, he could well be killed for bearing this unwelcome news. The other option was to keep his mouth shut. He would save his own neck, but it would cost the company millions. It also put them at a disadvantage with any competitor who had implemented the right solution at the right price.

My client faced a dilemma that is all too common today. From his perspective, there was a minute chance that he'd be recognized for doing the right thing by blowing the whistle, but it was even more likely that he'd be vilified.

I want to emphasize that this is hardly an isolated incident. I hear about this kind of thing happening all the time. Like my IT client, people are really torn, forced to choose between the company's welfare and their own. Yet, it's really a trap we've built for ourselves. If Playing Big is so discouraged and so rare in Corporate America, businesses will grow less and less competitive. Ironically, like in the previous example, operating costs will continue to go up—not down—as our competitive advantage continues to tank.

That's why I think it's essential for enlightened CEOs to foster an Emperor's No Clothes culture. For themselves, their workforce and the company's good, it's imperative that people know it's okay to blurt out that the Emperor's nude—if, for no other reason, than to halt big, expensive mistakes. In the previous example, if such a culture had been in place, they would not only have decreased cost, but also preserved their competitive advantage. But as long as companies support the other kind of culture—where Playing Big is not only frowned on but actively discouraged—it only fuels their race to the bottom.

You may be curious to know what path my IT client chose. In the end, he elected to preserve his job and take care of his family by keeping his mouth shut. It was a lose-lose outcome for him and the corporation. The tragedy is that no one should be put in his position, electing what he perceived as the lesser of two evils.

ALTERNATIVES—For those readers who are feeling stuck in a small culture and who desire to Play Big, there are a number of options.

I'll start by discussing the one that may seem most extreme, then proceed to suggest some things you could initiate right where you find yourself today.

LEAVING—The first option is to leave—to find another job. If you've already considered this, you've probably experienced a running commentary from the Lilliputians reminding you that you have obligations to your family, credit card bills and you might be making the biggest mistake of your life.

Here's where I think it's helpful to be realistic, but in a slightly different way. The reality check I'm referring to is that if your current situation has habituated you to playing small, the longer you remain there, the more unemployable you become. Imagine a regime change at your current workplace. A new boss comes on the scene. There's that inevitable face-to-face meeting with the new boss where you're invited to describe what you've achieved during your tenure. If you've been playing small, it will be a short, unimpressive list. As the new regime sorts who stays and who goes, without much to show for your years with the company, you end up in the out box. Yes, leaving is not without its risks, but staying and playing small is equally risky, if not more so.

If you're in this situation, don't blame yourself. Recognize it as conditioning. Like the baby elephant who is taught he can't, so he doesn't try.

I'm reminded here of how important it is to understand that Playing Big is really an all-or-nothing proposition. Even if you've remained in a job where you've managed to play a little less small than the next guy, what have you accomplished? There's a hollow ring to all small victories, like being the tallest Lilliputian. When it's time to list your accomplishments, you won't have many more than the next tallest Lilliputian.

Over time, we forget we are elephants, not Lilliputians. We forget that Playing Big was ever an option. My experience is that this is the very thing that drains the life and joy from people. Whenever I encounter someone who is stuck, this is why. They've quit on themselves. It's actually a form of self-betrayal, and it usually gives way to a "victimization" mind-set. Inevitably, you can only play small for so long before you begin to blame those around you for your smallness. This, in itself, is the stickiest of traps. Blaming others for what you're mired in is the surest way you'll stay there. You'll force yourself to wait for the people you're blaming to shape up—and they seldom do.

PICKING YOUR BATTLES—Some find it possible to occasionally Play Big in a small culture by picking their battles. From time to time, they'll identify issues or initiatives that they believe are worth fighting for, and they tiptoe into battle. Usually, they're looking for opportunities to rise to their full height where the upside clearly outweighs the downside. It's a form of risk taking, albeit a highly selective form. And it's problematic, as it can easily become a convenient rationalization for choosing to do nothing. Along the slippery slope of picking your battles, what frequently happens is that you pick very few or almost no battles at all, simply because it's hard to keep flicking this mind-set "on" and "off." Being Schwarzenegger in Terminator 2 one minute and Dora the Explorer the next, gets dizzying, and is another reminder that Playing Big favors an all-or-nothing commitment. Clearly, picking your battles requires you to compartmentalize yourself. Some rare individuals are able to pull it off, but most find it difficult to do, and the level of satisfaction will rarely justify the required effort.

CREATE YOUR OWN SUBCULTURE—Here's an approach that is a solid step up from picking your battles. I worked with some clients recently on creating their own subculture within a very large corporation. This four-person team wrote their own mission statement, setting a standard that potentially exceeds that of the corporation at large. This higher standard they chose to hold themselves to included things like exceptional performance, innovative creative output and the commitment to leap over boundaries in the pursuit of excellence. They went about as far as they could go with this, understanding that realistically they still had to operate within the corporation's parameters. But what's powerful is they created a team environment where they could celebrate the team's innovations and accomplishments. It made the team stronger. It gave them a focus and purpose that made it easier to get things done and put marks on the board. I've also seen this work very effectively when teams, even small ones, are divided over several locations.

These subcultures are effective for a number of reasons, not the least of which is that they fulfill a key desire for most of us—to feel like we're really part of something versus just another person in another beige cubicle. I've also seen these subcultures create a positive ripple effect throughout companies as other teams observe what's happening and move to create their own subculture. It renews hope among those who want to Play Big that, acknowledging the innocuousness of the larger culture, there actually is an alternative to the status quo.

Even if you're not part of a team, you can create your own—a subculture of one. What's helpful in this case is using an ally, which could be a mentor, coach, advisor or even your significant other. We've talked previously about the role of this ally in giving you someone to be accountable to. Being a culture of one has its challenges, but I still recommend it over the "picking your battles" alternative. Because even if it's only you (and your ally), you can remain in a Playing Big mind-set continuously. When you pick your battles, you Play Big intermittently and then easily fall back into playing small.

FINDING ALLIES: *The Close Encounters* Approach—Remember what happens in the movie *Close Encounters of the Third Kind*? Roy Neary (Richard Dreyfuss) has an extraterrestrial encounter. Full of doubts, he fears he may actually be going crazy until he begins to encounter others who also share his telltale radiation sunburn and similar contacts with those otherworldly beings. You can have the same "OMG—I've finally found my people!" realization when you begin to discover those who are like-minded within your company. Soul mates who, like you, are determined to Play Big no matter the odds. These like-minded encounters can take on several constructive forms. At a minimum, people can bond together for mutual support, keeping the home fires burning in a culture that doesn't encourage Playing Big. And they can collaborate, seizing opportunities to work together on projects much as a small team or subculture would do.

ENTREPRENEURSHIP—Here's a critical question I challenge you to ask yourself: if you're currently in a job where you're counting steps between the land mines, how much riskier can it be to leave and do something else? Look at Microsoft. Hundreds of unhappy campers there decided to pick up their laptops and take a hike, forming successful companies on their own. Those who choose the entrepreneurial route have a key advantage: their willingness to Play Big. They've shown that they can succeed over monoliths like Microsoft. Who, as they grow, begin to fear Playing Big. The competitive advantage entrepreneurs hold over the giants is they can be bolder and more nimble. Which, in the technology industry, for example, can mean everything. They also have access to the same resources as their fat competitors, thanks to globalization. As many companies sit back, cut costs and shelve innovation, they hand would-be entrepreneurs a better-than-average chance of success, notwithstanding a tough economy.

Nowhere is this entrepreneurial drive more evident than in the advertising industry. Consider that the majority of top-tier ad agencies today didn't exist 20 years ago. It represents what's frequently the sad cycle in this industry: a very creative ad shop opens up, they do great work, but as the agency grows, the creative work becomes less and less risky until it is indistinguishable from all the other annoying, ineffective advertising. Eventually, the real creative talent gets tired of being a Lilliputian, takes a walk and a new agency is born. Even Jay Chiat, the legendary ad mogul behind Chiat Day—builder of brands like Apple and Nissan—was circumspect enough to say with respect to their expansion, "Let's see how big we can get before we get bad." He obviously knew the biggest danger to a successful and growing ad agency was playing safe and small.

Neil Simon wrote a wonderful play called Brighton Beach Memoirs, a humorous chronicle of the Jerome family's efforts to survive the Great Depression. At one point in the play, Stanley confesses to his brother Eugene that he was fired from his job. When Eugene asks if the firing is permanent, Stanley replies, "You don't get fired temporarily. It's a permanent lifetime firing." The Lilliputians couldn't have said it better.

PLAYING BIGGER:

1. In Sync—Make a list of the values that are most important to you, (e.g. "honesty," "sense of humor," etc.). Then look at your reality, including work life, family life, etc. Are the two in sync? In what areas? Are there other areas where your cherished values and your daily reality are miles apart?

2. Getting Unstuck—If you feel that you're a Big Player who is stuck in a small culture, use the discussion of options in this book to brainstorm ways to get yourself unstuck.

CHAPTER 8 – LEAVING A BIG LEGACY

"Never, never, never give up."
—Winston Churchill

LEGENDARY AVIATOR AMELIA EARHART once commented that some people are lucky enough to have great runways built for them. She said if that's your case, you should take off! But if you don't have a runway, recognize that it's your responsibility to pick up a shovel and build one—not only for yourself but for those who will fly after you.

Earhart's quote reminds me of the guy to whom I owe much, whose vision and commitment to never, never give up inspired me to Play Big. A guy who started out without a shovel, much less a runway. His name is Rasheen Coleman.

His mother was addicted to drugs. She abused Rasheen both mentally and physically. Since he was 6 years old, he was responsible for the care of his two younger half-siblings. When he was nine, Rasheen's mother died of AIDS. But he had a dream that was so much bigger than his circumstances, and he went on to graduate from a top-ranked prep school, then Morehouse College, and ultimately, the prestigious Bush School of Government. And in 1997, Rasheen Coleman was named Boys & Girls Clubs of America's National Youth of the Year.

In terms of inspiring my own Playing Big, Rasheen was my Roger Bannister. And once Rasheen "broke the record," rising above his challenges to reach success, I began to ask myself, "If that's possible for him, what's possible for me?" His achievement had thrown down a gauntlet that made me seriously consider if I was playing as big as I could—and by his example, I realized that I could be playing way, *way* bigger.

For me, Rasheen's story frames this conversation on legacy perfectly, because when you choose to Play Big in your life, you create a legacy. It just happens, whether you intend it to or not. I think about how many people Rasheen and his story have touched, often in very profound ways. I know personally of at least a hundred in his hometown alone who stand witness to his Playing Big experience. As National Youth of the Year, he spoke all over the country. Now we're getting into the exponential effect—many of those people told his story to more people, who told more people and so on. If the rock you throw into the pond is big enough and you throw it with everything you've got, the ripples go out and out and never stop.

The first field where Rasheen inspired me to Play Big was Omaha's Boys and Girls Clubs, where I was serving on the Board of Directors. We knew from market research that we were serving only 10% of the kids who could benefit from our programs. Our membership was around 4,500 at the time. To reach a significantly larger number of youth in the Omaha metropolitan area seemed insanely ambitious. But we chose to follow that path, inspired in large part by Rasheen's optimism, to mount a capital campaign we called "2X"—named to communicate our goal of doubling not only our current membership but also doubling our facilities.

In hindsight, Playing Big in this case meant not only success; it ensured survival. The recession of 2007 hit. Nearly all the capital campaigns of other non-profits in the area were being shelved. Because our dream was so outrageous and we didn't quit, we were able to capture the imagination of our donors. Through their generosity, and notwithstanding uncertain economic times, we significantly increased both the Clubs' membership and facilities, and came through the downturn much better than most other non-profit organizations.

That Rasheen wasn't afraid to dream—and dream big—had inspired us to create a legacy of our own.

When I examine Rasheen's amazing story and the process that got him from where he began to where he is today, I see two important steps: a Big Dream, and then a Big Plan.

A BIG DREAM—Having a Big Dream is the first, most important thing. When Rasheen declared he wanted to one day attend this prestigious prep school, it sounded outrageous. At the time, he was struggling to maintain decent grades in his public school, but there's something about having an outrageous goal that does what a realistic goal cannot. It inspires you to go beyond the known realm of your own capabilities. It captures the interest and imagination of others in a way that a smaller and more reasonable goal cannot. The litmus of a Big Dream is that it must send chills down your spine—and ideally down the spines of everyone in your vicinity. Just thinking about it must be awe-inspiring to you. It must be for you to break free from the gravitational pull of staying put and the bondage of the Lilliputians we discussed in earlier chapters.

All of Rasheen's goals—from getting into prep school to being named National Youth of the Year—seemed to lie on the ragged edge of ridiculous. I would argue this was a huge part of his success. If he'd set his sights lower—say his goal was just to pass English in his local public school—not only would it not have been big enough for him, but it also wouldn't have been big enough for those around him who would become part of his legacy. Getting crystal clear on the "what" is so important, and in many ways, that big choice was 99% responsible for his success.

After stating your Big Dream, I realize now that what follows is a lot of nuts and bolts tasks. But getting the dream right should take precedence, and should make you ring like a tuning fork whenever you consider it. It should kindle a sense of wonder, like hanging your toes over the edge and peering down into the Grand Canyon. And it should inspire tremendous momentum, causing you to act in a way that's superior to the way you'd behave in the face of a much smaller goal.

When I ask my clients to write this all-important "What" statement, I lay out the criteria: does it really inspire you? Is it big enough? Is it thrilling? Is it at least somewhat terrifying? However you label your own special energy—your chi or prana or the Holy Spirit—your Big Dream must engage that energy. Rasheen had several Big Dreams. Whether he realized it or not, the size of his dreams provided the key to keeping him inspired and engaged and made him bounce out of bed each morning toward their fulfillment. And there's another truism about Playing Big: when you do it, you never play alone. Your ability to activate that energy within, to ring like that tuning fork, will resonate with everyone within earshot of your Big Dream.

A BIG PLAN—On the heels of a Big Dream must come a Big Plan. In Rasheen's case, his plan was created with help from others—a trusted set of allies to whom he simply said, "Here's what I want to do. Now, I need you to tell me how."

Here come the "nuts and bolts" I referred to earlier in the chapter. Rasheen got some really good advice early in the pursuit of his goal. If he wanted to get into this prep school, he would first need to excel in his current school. He'd need a tutor to accomplish this, so that his grades would reach a level that made him a good candidate for admission to the prep school. And more tutoring to help him pass the actual admissions test.

Rasheen dove in, unaware that his legacy had begun. The prep school bought into his dream and got involved. They invested in his success. No matter how much the Lilliputians try to persuade us otherwise, when you let go of your fear and declare what you want to do, helping hands always appear. A Big Plan begins to emerge. Rasheen didn't do much to author his plan. It was created around him by people who were inspired by what he was doing and wanted to do it with him.

Rasheen's example also demonstrates how easy it is, once you have declared your "impossible" goal, to explode that goal into a lot of possible steps. His steps included "Meet with my tutor after school" and "Study each night from 7 p.m. until 10 p.m." The magic occurs at both stages—conceiving the Big Dream, and then transitioning to the Big Plan that contains all the steps to make it happen. And, if necessary, to keep exploding the impossible dream into smaller and smaller pieces that look possible.

In pursuit of his dream, Rasheen was equipped with a couple of things that will serve you well too. First, he was willing to approach the whole thing with complete humility. He recognized in his heart that what he was attempting seemed impossible. This humility made it easy for him to ask for and receive help. As antithetical as it sounds, humbling himself to his Big Dream made him more powerful in its pursuit.

The other thing he did, which is somewhat an antecedent to his humility, is that he agreed to be fully accountable as he went after his dream—to his advisors, to those who were watching and admiring his efforts, and most importantly, to himself. He knew that in the end, the victory or the failure would rest squarely on his shoulders, and he would accept that. No blame allowed.

Once your Big Dream and Big Plan are both on the table, there's another component that's critical: your Big Commitment. I love that quote of Churchill's that kicks off this chapter. It's that stick-to-itiveness that is the defining difference. With your plan, you've begun to turn the impossible into the possible. But you will inevitably also experience resistance, the instinctive pull to remain at homeostasis, from the Lilliputians and other detractors who'd rather see you stay right where you are. So, to make a commitment that you will *never, never, never give up* is essential. Rasheen made this commitment. I know there were many times when every fiber of his soul was stretched to the breaking point. But he had made a sacred pact, and he never gave up.

Commitment isn't just essential. It's really the thing that ensures your success. When employed 100%, commitment literally converts the impossible into a sure thing. If the dream and the plan are right, and we can commit to never giving up, then we can turn something that looks like it would take a miracle into something that now seems inevitable.

Another factor in Rasheen's success was that he didn't come at this from an adult's perspective—from a point of view that could have made him overly aware of how crazy he was to tackle a dream of this magnitude. He dreamed as kids do—with abandon—but there was nothing childish about his sense of responsibility. He knew that a lot of people were pulling for him and cheering him on, and he was not about to let either them or himself down. He was able to bring his words and actions together in complete alignment.

The huge commitment Rasheen made was reflective of his character. He's a guy who simply does not give up. That kind of persistence can cover a multitude of sins. We put so much emphasis on talent, but talent does not have to be the determining factor for Playing Big. Or, as Calvin Coolidge once said, "...nothing is more common than unsuccessful men with talent." In fact, when you make the kind of commitment Rasheen made to your Big Dream, you will discover gifts within you that you never knew existed. We're not talking about making some big miracle. We're talking about doing a lot of small, possible things each day and keeping faith that the miraculous sum will be exponentially greater than the parts. And when you make that kind of commitment—as Rasheen did—you create the engine that drives everything.

Rasheen's legacy, in effect, created itself. While he focused on the task, hundreds watched. The unit directors and staff at the local Boys & Girls Club, the Club's board of directors, and particularly, the other kids at the Club. In Rasheen, they all saw their own dreams and desires. I point this out because we tend to think of a legacy as something that is revealed after someone has passed on, but for Rasheen, that legacy began the moment he said his Big Dream out loud.

The same was true for Roger Bannister. In the quest to break a four-minute mile, his legacy began not when he finally breasted that ribbon at the finish line to break the record, but several years before, when he announced his intention to do so. From that moment, he started capturing the imagination of other athletes and eventually the world. Consciously or not, he was doing something that was much bigger than he was. When you're after a Big Dream, you're not just doing it for yourself. You ignite hope and inspiration within everyone who watches. And you acquire a bigger responsibility, bigger than yourself, to never give up. You hold in your hands an ability to remind us what humans are capable of when we commit to Playing Big.

Big Dream. Big Plan. Big Commitment. Big Responsibility. The responsibility of all this becomes quite profound when you appreciate how many people can be pulled into the wake of our Big Dreams. Both Roger Bannister and Rasheen Coleman saw its effect. It's a phenomenon that transcends the dream itself. At this level, it's risen beyond whether somebody gets into a prep school or breaks a track and field record. It's about tapping into an energy that's so much greater than we are. If we can access that force, anything is possible.

Our tendency is to consider ourselves separate from that rare class of big dreamers, men like Steve Jobs or Martin Luther King. And yet, everyone, no matter how much talent they think they have or have been told they have, has a real opportunity to have and act on a Big Dream and to inspire everyone around them in a big way.

There's an enormous responsibility in Playing Big. There's also a big debt. By that, I mean that one of the best ways we can show gratitude for this opportunity to be alive and for our gifts—and we all have many—is to Play Big. To take our life and our gifts as far as we can, not only for the personal rewards, but also for how it can change our families, our community and the world around us.

Bertold Brecht, the German playwright and poet, offered this cautionary line: "Do not fear death so much, but rather the inadequate life." A life based on fear is just that—inadequate. A life based on Playing Big is miles beyond adequate. It's daring to dream, and making that dream reality. It's taking everything we've got and running with everything we've got. And creating a legacy that starts immediately and never ends.

PLAYING BIGGER:

1. Your Big Dream—If you've had one in the back of your mind, now is the time to write it down. Say it out loud. How does it feel? Now that you've expressed it, what fears come up as you think about pursuing it?

2. Tracking a Legacy—Identify a person, either living or from history, that left a significant legacy. Can you identify a ripple effect—unintended consequences of Playing Big that this person could not have imagined? Based on your Big Dream, what would you like your legacy to be?

INTERVIEWS

AUTHOR'S NOTE: I've included some interviews here, edited slightly for clarity, of people who I have had the great privilege to witness as they Play Big in their own lives. Up to this point, I've given you a lot of words on this Playing Big phenomenon. But I believe what speaks loudest is the testimony of people like these—ordinary people with extraordinary courage to change their lives and, in the process, the lives of everyone around them.

S.A.

CARRIE DUFFY

Ten years ago, Carrie was a successful commercial real estate broker. She had a great income, and had finally moved into the home of her dreams—a country ranch with stables for the horses she loved. But she was miserable, still working in an environment where she knew in her gut she didn't belong. She took a risk, made the switch to selling agricultural properties, and is today vice president of Mid-Continent Properties, Inc., where her affinity for agribusiness and land development has finally come home. Our Playing Big interviewer caught up with Carrie on her ranch recently and asked her to discuss her big change.

PB: *Can you remember a particular moment when you knew you needed to get out, to make a change?*

CD: There were probably two moments. There was the moment I knew in my heart I needed to make the change but wasn't willing to take the action. Then there was the moment I knew I had to make a change—it was a life-or-death situation in my mind, and I was willing to take the next step and engage a coach. I knew I needed to make a change and was willing to listen at that point.

My goal in life was to earn enough money at what I was doing that I could eventually have a place in the country, where I could have horses on my property and live the lifestyle I felt I was destined to live. And I did that, and then when I got there, and I walked out the door in the morning to go to work in commercial real estate, I realized I was finally where I was meant to be, but I was only part-way there. Because I was still working in a place that didn't match where I lived and what I really loved. And I knew then, oh my gosh, it's going to be so hard to continue down this professional path, having reached this goal, living where I want to live, but the one component that's still not right is where I'm spending my professional life—which is a big part of your life. But I also felt like financially I needed to stay on at that place to sustain what I had achieved. And it was between seven and ten years later that I lost five very close friends in a matter of two-and-a-half years. The first to cancer, and the youngest of which was 42.

PB: *It does make you think …*

CD: Yeah, yeah—and I had a mammogram come back suspicious. And two of those friends I had lost to breast cancer. And my first thought was, "If I'm one of these unlucky ones that I've just watched lose the battle, and I know now having watched them that my time might be less than I had envisioned, what's the first thing I'd change?"

And it was instantaneous: it was my career. That was absolute. And that was enough motivation to spend some money, spend some time, whatever it took to make a change. Because we all know life is short, and every day we leave, we never know if today's our last. But when you're really faced with thinking in those terms, either because of life experiences, or because of something that's just thrown at you as a scary moment, then you re-evaluate how you want to spend your time. And thankfully, (the mammogram) turned out fine. And you know the other thing I went to is if there's something in my life that's toxic and that's going to undermine my health, what is it? And it was my profession.

PB: *I've known a lot of people in that business, and it's really high stress. And at a certain point, even if your commissions are great—it sounds like what you're saying is that when you look at the cost, is it really worth it?*

CD: Yeah ... and I knew ... no, I guess I should say I thought I knew it was high stress and I hate to use these terms, but cutthroat, and a highly competitive environment. But when you're in it every day, you kind of lose perspective on that. And I would go to a place of, "I just need to toughen up," or "These other people seem to be doing it and it doesn't seem to bother them—why does it bother me? I'm a freak." But since I've been out of it, I find it amazing when other people like you say it's stressful, because when you're in it, it's hard to realize really. And I think that's true of any situation. I don't care if it's a bad relationship or whatever, or if you have some illness, you don't realize how bad it is until you're removed from it.

PB: *And it's amazing what we can adapt to—like it's our nature as human beings to be highly adaptable.*

CD: Right. So that was my moment when I decided to take the next step. And I don't think it was any mistake that I knew somebody who knew Scott and what he was doing, and I think they had told me before I had reached that point. But I was able to go back to them and say, I'm really at a point where I want to meet with him and try and figure this out.

PB: And what was that first meeting like?

CD: Well, I knew Scott, but certainly not as well as I know him now. After the first meeting I thought, "We didn't talk about any of the things I thought we were going to talk about." I thought it was going to be all about goals, and financial goals, and all the things that you're being driven to when you're going to make a change or achieve something different. And it was a lot about how I felt when I was where I was at, and how I felt when I was in those fleeting moments when I was where I thought I should be, where I found the greatest joy in life. And then we talked a lot about faith. A lot about faith. And I say this totally tongue-in-cheek, because I felt it was the bait-and-switch, it was like he was going to make this so easy (laughs). I'm just gonna pay him, and he's gonna do it, and say, "Here's where you're supposed to be!"

PB: Like, "I hired this independent contractor, and he's going to take care of it ..."

CD: Yeah (laughing)—like he was just going to tell me what color my next office was going to be!

PB: Exactly. "Just let me know when to show up, and ..."

CD: But it was not that way.

PB: *Looking back, what do you think really carried you over the hump? It was challenging, right, because you had worked yourself up to a certain level in your career, and nobody likes to start over, regardless of what that pot of gold seems like at the end of the rainbow. What do you think kept you Playing Big through the tougher parts?*

CD: The tougher parts of the process of changing?

PB: *Yeah. You knew it wasn't going to happen overnight, but at the six-month mark, or the one-year mark, when you're still spending your savings, what kept you going and motivated?*

CD: Well, part of making the change was changing who I was working with. Not only did I change career paths to a certain degree—I mean I'm still doing real estate, but in an entirely different environment and a whole different product line. But it was the new people that I was associated with in my day-to-day business. Their priorities and values just matched mine to a much greater degree. And they were so encouraging! They kept telling me, "You're doing great!" And I thought, "Well, I sure don't see it financially." But it was their encouragement, and the fact that I was now in an environment where the values matched my own. And that gave me the strength, encouragement and faith to hang in there.

PB: *Can you recall a moment when, at last, you finally felt this new direction was going to work out?*

CD: Well, I can tell you—and this is kind of bizarre—when I was in commercial real estate, I was always operating from a place of tremendous insecurity and fear. Fear that I wasn't going to do as well as people expected me to, fear that there was going to be a backlash of some kind. And after I changed and was in this other position for a while, I remember doing a pitch to get some business or I was negotiating something, and I was now coming from a place of such tremendous confidence. And I was looking around like, "Where is this coming from?" because I know less about what I'm doing now by far than what I was doing before. But I am coming from such a place of confidence, and have so much self-assurance that I never seemed to be able to achieve after twenty-some years in that other line of work.

PB: *Exactly!*

CD: It was such a gift, and it was like, "Gee!" And you know what, that came through to people. They wanted to do business with me because I was confident. I was very optimistic about how things were going to go.

PB: *It's that old thing about believing in the product. And the product was you.*

CD: Exactly. Our product is all relationship-based.

PB: *Just curious, do you still encounter any of the people from your former life in commercial real estate sales?*

CD: Yeah, and the timing of that question is pretty interesting, because I just went a week ago Friday to a one-day commercial real estate conference. I needed some continuing education, and this particular conference satisfied that. But all the people I used to do business with were there. And I was really disappointed... and this is just something I'm going to have to work on. I was really disappointed about how anxious I got when I was going. And I was like, "Why am I so nervous about this?" I didn't have to get up there—I wasn't on some panel. In years past, I might have been somebody on one of the panels.

PB: *I guess it's our nature that those situations tend to dredge up all those feelings ...*

CD: It was just like a blast from the past. And everything came rolling back.

PB: *But after you got beyond that, wasn't there some satisfaction in thinking that they're all still there and you've moved on—and moved on in a pretty big way?*

CD: Yeah. And I had a number of people ask me, "Did you get into agricultural property sales because you knew the commercial market was going to tank and agriculture was going to take off?" And I'd love to think I'm that smart, but I know I'm not. It was just the luck of the draw. When I say that, I love this definition of luck I read a long time ago—that it's when preparedness meets opportunity. And I was certainly prepared to make a change. And when the opportunity presented itself, a lot of things fell into place in the way they were supposed to, and I was lucky that I made the move when I did. Because everything cycles.

PB: *So how do you plan to keep Playing Big and build on the success you've already experienced?*

CD: You know, I'm really expanding my networking opportunities in the agricultural world. I got this from the process of Playing Big, because the possibilities now seem limitless, where before my vision was a lot narrower. I don't know that where I'm sitting at my desk today is the end of the path. I think I'm on the right path, but I don't know that this is the end. And to that extent, I've become involved in ag-related networking groups where I'm not only talking about real estate, but implement dealerships and environmental issues. It's cattlemen and anything that's remotely related. I do believe that I'm supposed to be in some ag-related business. Whether it remains the real estate end of it, I don't know. I don't know what God's got in store for me. But I do know that these are the kind of people, this is the kind of environment that I'm meant to be in. But maybe that path means that I'll end up going to work for someone in some ancillary line of business. And to that extent, I'm leaving tomorrow to meet with some people in Tulsa that own hotels, of all things, office buildings, apartments—a lot of the stuff I came from on the commercial side, but they also own some pretty large ranching operations. So what I hope in being able to meet with them is to be able to showcase what I know—which was the commercial real estate side, so I speak their language. But the fact that they have some large cattle and ranching operations means that they are also very committed to the ag side of things. So, I'm going to go down to meet with them because there may be an opportunity to do some business with these people. I have no idea what that will look like. And before I went through this Playing Big process, I really had to be able to visualize what something was going to look like before I was willing to step out there. And now I can go, not really having any preconceived idea of what it's going to look like or what the end result will be. Just go in there, make the contacts, meet the people and leave the rest up to how it will be.

PB: *Was that your background? Did you grow up in an agricultural environment?*

CD: No, no! I grew up in midtown Omaha. Attended high school in South Omaha. But I remember in high school meeting with the guidance counselor and talking about college. And he was saying, "Well, where do you want to go?" And I said I wanted to go to South Dakota and study agriculture. He looked at me like I had two heads because he wondered, "Where is this coming from?" I knew I loved horses, I knew I loved being outside, but my dad was a bricklayer. And I got no encouragement in that direction. But what I found out much later was somebody did our family tree and studied the family genealogy, and that my dad's side of the family came over from Ireland. A bunch of them settled in eastern Iowa and were all farmers. It was like gosh, maybe it was just in my veins, just really in my makeup.

PB: *But I love all that because it speaks to the idea that there is an inner voice in everybody, and it's amazing how, particularly when you're in high school, you're so susceptible to influence.*

CD: I liken it to when you're a first-time parent. You have all these little inner voices telling you something's wrong, but then your physician or your grandma says everything's fine. But you know there's something wrong, and it turns out there is something wrong. That was my experience with having children. You feel like you're born with something maternal, that my gut was telling me things. I think that's one of the great things about getting older is that I'm not as afraid to listen to what my gut says anymore.

PB: *Well, that's all great stuff—anything else? Any advice for others who want to be Playing Bigger in their lives, who might now be where you were 10 years ago when this whole thing started for you?*

CD: I'm friends with someone who is in a very similar position of how I felt prior to making a change, so I now get to look and say, "Wow, I know way too well how this feels." I don't think she believes me when I try to talk to her about some of the stuff, because apparently she's not ready. But the one thing she is coming around to, that I think would be good advice for anybody in that position, is that we have that inner voice, and one thing that drowns that out more effectively than anything is being around those people that are coming from a place of their own fear—or they have very self-limiting beliefs. Because I can get really sucked into that if I'm not careful, if I don't see that for what it is. Some of it I guess is just aligning yourself with those people that are going to encourage you. Another thing is that there's always risk in making a change, but it's a more calculated risk, and I think that's something Scott's good at—helping you quantify some of the risk. You don't want that to be what limits you, but he helps you quantify it.

PB: *And maybe what is real, tangible risk and what's only a risk in your mind?*

CD: Exactly. Like asking yourself, "What's the worst thing that could happen?" They might get mad at you? Wow!

PB: *People do get mad—it happens.*

CD: (laughing) That's right! The only other thing I would say is, this change for me took place three-plus years ago now, and I realize that everybody moves through this process at a different pace. When Scott and I first took this on, we were going to get it done in six weeks. It took me six months. It just took me longer to process some of these things. So, I think you have to be gentle with yourself when you go through this, and know that no two people are going to do it exactly the same. You certainly don't want to compare yourself to anybody else that way. But the other thing is that when this all took place my kids were 16, 15 and 12. So they were just going through the process of finishing up school and thinking about college, and my thinking about what was possible for them really opened up. My idea of what their possibilities were changed dramatically when I began exploring my own possibilities. So, I think my kids today are in a much better place as far as thinking beyond, whether it was their guidance counselor, or the influence of their friends, or even where I might have been had I not done this. I think we would have been a lot more worried about, "Oh my gosh, you want to study abroad—are you kidding? How are we going to pay for that?" This has just taken me so beyond all of those things, not just for myself, but for the people around me and my kids especially.

PB: It's an amazing story—thanks for sharing it.

CD: Oh, thank you!

RASHEEN COLEMAN

At 34, Rasheen's story already reads like the screenplay for a major motion picture. Abused and neglected as the child of a drug-addicted mother who died of AIDS when he was nine, he nevertheless found a way out. His way out led him first to a prestigious boys prep school, then to Morehouse College, and finally to graduate work at the Bush School of Government. After success in Washington, D.C., he's now in St. Louis working in the non-profit sector. Our interviewer had an opportunity to speak with him recently and talk about his life so far and to learn that part of Playing Big is having the courage to start over.

PB: *I'm always amazed at guys like you who had so many challenges growing up, and still you came out on top. Then there are also kids who were fed with a silver spoon and wind up on drugs, alcohol and other bad things. How do you account for this?*

RC: I have two different viewpoints on it. First, having someone to mentor you. I think mentorship is vital to anyone—whether you come from a good background or a horrible one. You need someone to see something in you that you can't see yet yourself. And that's what happened for me at the Boys & Girls Club. I was confused. I was hurt. I was withdrawn. I don't think people expected much of me. Even my aunt, who raised me, thought I would lose my mind one day, or I would be suicidal. And to have those words spoken to me as a little kid really hurt my feelings. But I had people in my life who believed in me. People who saw that leadership ability in me and nurtured it by putting positive things into my life. They made resources available for me—for example, to go to Creighton Prep, to go to Morehouse College; and just having someone to guide you along, to help you discover you. They don't tell you who you are per se, but they let you know what you have in you so you sit back and think, "Hmm, with this leadership training I could do this, or with that, I can help change not only my life, but my family's life, and I can change the future. I can change the vibe across the world—to think globally." And the other side of that is some people just know what they want, they have this drive in them, they've experienced so many negative things that they have this drive to be better and do better. And that inspires them to make the right choices and the right decisions to align themselves with the people and the organizations that help prepare them for their destiny.

PB: *And you're saying that was you?*

RC: I think it was a combination of both. I just saw how my mother treated me—the person who should have loved me the most rejected me, abused me. And I didn't want that for my future kids, and I didn't want that for myself. I didn't want to deal with substance abuse, or mental illness. I wanted to succeed. I didn't want poor decisions to destroy me. And I had that drive. I said, "Okay, I see." Boys & Girls Clubs had shown me I can be a leader. I developed my own Torch newsletter at the age of 12. And then I became a leader in the Keystone Club, and I decided that, "Hey, I wanna change people's lives. I want to go into politics!" (laughs) So I majored in political science, and eventually settled on urban studies and public administration. I realized that I wanted to be a change-maker. I wanted to be what some people call "a troublemaker of the best kind." And just follow my dream. So I had both—the nature and the nurture, as they would call it.

PB: *And you had some heavy responsibilities that most kids don't have at that age. Taking care of your younger siblings.*

RC: Yeah, it amazes me. When I look at when my mother died, I guess it was around 1988, I think I was nine or ten, just looking back at the time when she was drugged out ... I was brushing my sister's hair, and we were walking to school, and my brother wasn't old enough to go to school so he was left with my mother. Just thinking back about that, "Wow, I had to take care of my brother and sister and I was only nine years old." Looking back now, it seems like another lifetime. It just amazes me.

PB: *Can you think of a particular time during your childhood when it hit you that you somehow just had to get out of there, like "If I keep going on like this, I'm not gonna make it"?*

RC: We went through various foster homes, but we were always returned to our mother, because the foster care system would rather you be with your parents. And sometimes that's not good if they're not ready to take care of the kids.

There was a point when I must have really had something going on in my mind, because a voice told me, "Just kill her." I could see myself taking a knife and going into my mother's room and stabbing her in her sleep. But, thank God, for some reason that didn't happen. What did happen is I realized, "I can't take any more of this, I can't take this any longer." So I ran away. My mother had sworn to beat me for something, so I ran away to my great-grandmother's house. I ran all the way from my house. I don't know how I knew how to get there, but I did.

I stayed with my great-grandmother for a while, and that's when we found out that my mother had HIV. She could have had AIDS at the time, because she died within a year, I believe.

PB: *Sounds like there was plenty of pain there.*

RC: Yeah, I had a lot of hatred for my mother, because I was the only one she abused. She neglected us because she was a drug addict, but I was the only one she physically abused. That hurt me. And people would say, "Well, your mother's sick," but that didn't pacify me or make me feel better. I just saw it as an excuse. I kept saying no, there was a reason behind this. I don't know if she was mad at my biological father or with me because I never wanted to live with her. She gave me away at birth, and I ended up in Mobile, Ala. She came and kidnapped me at the age of six, and that was the first of two times she kidnapped me. And then she abused me.

And so throughout the years, trying to develop relationships, I thought I would never get married. I felt like I didn't have a capacity to receive love and had a limited capacity to give love—to anyone. I cared about people, but if they brought their problems to me, I felt mine were just enormous compared to theirs, even though there were other people who were abused far worse than I was. But at the time, it was all about the interpretation, about how I felt. So I went through therapy off and on from the age of 6 until 16. It wasn't very useful for me, because I wasn't really ready to talk about it. It wasn't until I went to therapy before I got married that I started to understand some things and could put things in the proper perspective.

PB: *And the process of your education …*

RC: When it comes to the process of my education, and trusting people, the Boys & Girls Club took me under their wing. They said, "Creighton Prep is coming to the South Omaha Boys & Girls Club for an informational session, and we want you to sit in." And I was thinking, "Okay, you want me to go to Creighton Prep, with all these rich white kids? I'm a little black kid from the projects! Yeah, right!" (laughs) That's what I was thinking. So they came and the Boys & Girls Club was like, "We'll help you with your books and it would be a great opportunity for you—you're doing well at Bryan Junior High." And I'm thinking I could go to Bryan High or South High and get easy As and Bs, so why should I go to Creighton Prep? And barely survive, in my eyes.

But I took the risk. I went. I did okay my freshman year. I failed one class—world history. But they were like, "Just try it for one year. If you don't like it, then you can leave." But by then, I'd already made friends. And I passed, so I could do the work. So I'm like, "I'm staying here." So I did work study, I worked at Wendy's in high school, and went to school. And I was able to do it.

I didn't have the best grades, I had a 2.5 maybe or 2.6, I don't know. I was able to get a full ride to the University of Nebraska at Omaha on the Goodrich Scholarship. And I had only applied to schools in Nebraska because I really didn't want to leave my family. So I got into UNL and Creighton and UNO, but UNO offered the most money, so I went there. And it was through the Boys & Girls Clubs that I got an internship with Gateway Computers in South Dakota. I spent two summers there. And that was a great experience in itself, to be away for two summers. Then while I was doing my internship at Gateway, Susan Whitfield from the Boys & Girls Club called me and said,

"You should consider going to Morehouse." I think we'd had a previous conversation about it. And I said, "You know what, I have a full ride here. If I go to Morehouse, they're not going to give me a full ride because I'll be a transfer student." I thought they wouldn't give me these scholarship opportunities as a transfer student. And she said, "Well, you need to step out on faith." And when she said that, I knew I couldn't say no. And I thought, "Wow, you're supposed to be a person of faith—how can you say no?" And the Boys & Girls Clubs' board of directors raised some money for me to go, and said, "Once you get there, you'll find the money. Yes, you'll have to take some loans, but a lot of people have to take loans." So I went to Morehouse.

It was a great experience. My first year there, I passed the bulletin board at Financial Aid, and I saw a scholarship with the United Negro College Fund, and with the Audubon Society and CSX. And I would be called a CSX Scholar. So I just had to apply, and they would pay you $14,000 per year, and they would give you an internship for two years. So I said, "Hmm… well, let me apply." I got the scholarship! And that paid for a big chunk of my $20,000 tuition. So that was like, "Wow!" I stepped out on faith, and this opportunity came. I seized upon it, and I got it! So I did an internship with the U.S. Department of Transportation in D.C., and I did one at the CSX Corporation in Jacksonville, Fla. So that worked out.

I was in my political science class about the time I was thinking about graduate school, and I saw this poster that said, "The George Bush School of Public Service—Do You Want To Be A Public Servant? Do You Want To Give Back?" You know, I think that was in 2000, and I was still upset about the 2000 election, and I said, "The Bush School?!"

But I said, "Well, let me take this postcard ..." and I mailed it off. Then the Boys & Girls Clubs of America called me and said they wanted me to go to this education summit in Atlanta. I was already in Atlanta, so I said, "Sure." And I was on this panel—we talked about the challenges of being in college, and we talked about exams and everything. So after the panel was over, a gentleman came up to me and said, "What do you want to do after Morehouse?" And I said, "I want to go to the Bush School." And he said to me, "Oh, really? I have a meeting with them next week." His name was Ron Rolett, and he was the president of the Boys & Girls Clubs of the Brazos Valley in Texas, which is located right next to the Bush School in College Station, Texas. He said, "Give me your information. I want you to be our emcee at our scholarship dinner. I can fly you down, and you can stay with one of the staff members. And I'll set up a meeting with you and some of the administration officials over there (at the Bush School)."

So he flew me down, I met with some of the officials, and they gave me a tour of the university. Because of that, not only was I accepted to the Bush School, I received the George Herbert Walker Bush Fellowship. So I got a full ride plus a stipend every month. And I was like, "Wow, this is just amazing!" And I was a little apprehensive, like how well will I do on the GRE—I hadn't done that well on the ACT. But I studied beforehand, and I did pretty well, so everything really fell into place. I could have said, "I don't want to go to that Republican school," or, "I'm not good enough," but I stepped out there and I went. I said, "Oh, they're going to see all this Democratic stuff on my resume. They're not going to let me in here!" But I stepped out on faith, and it all worked out. You know, to be successful, you have to take a lot of chances. You can't stay in your own zone. You can't have a fear of the unknown, because most of us have that, like we don't know what's going to happen. So we play it safe. But sometimes you have to Play Big and put yourself out there, be confident in who you are and your skills. And you can't let your past dictate your future.

PB: *There must have been a lot of moments like that when you asked yourself, "Is this for real? Is this really happening to me?"*

RC: Especially when I said, "I want to go to the Bush School," and he said, "I have a meeting with them next week." What?! (laughs) I mean, he just came out of the crowd, there were hundreds of people there at this summit. It was just amazing.

PB: *I guess if that doesn't make you believe in a higher power, what would?*

RC: I know.

PB: *Well, you've clearly been Playing Big for quite some time now.*

RC: You know, one of my favorite quotes is—and I found this one when I was National Youth of the Year for Boys & Girls Clubs—"Adversity causes some people to break, but it causes other people to break records." I thought that was so profound as it pertained to my life. Adversity could have taken me out. I could have been a substance abuser. I could have been in jail. Committed suicide—which I thought about as a child. That's a little scary, isn't it? Not even as a teenager, but as a child—to have contemplated suicide. But to be the first person from the Boys & Girls Clubs of Omaha to become National Youth of the Year. Then breaking the record of being the first in my family to obtain a bachelor's degree, and then a master's degree.

PB: *And you never stopped. I mean, you could have been happy just having gone to Creighton Prep and gotten into UNO. But you kept reaching for that next thing.*

RC: It's like Oprah said, as a young person, she knew she had this great destiny before her. And right now, even in my life, I feel destiny calling me. I'm 34, and I still feel that there are greater things for me. So I had a great job in D.C., high-paying job, but it wasn't exactly what I wanted to do. So I took the risk and moved down to St. Louis with my family, to be closer to my extended family and start over. So right now I'm playing it kind of small, but really I'm Playing Big, because I had to start out in an entry-level position at this organization that I'm in. I've been there less than 30 days, and I was called into the office a couple of days ago, and they're saying, "It's time for a promotion—we want you in this area." And now I'm starting to see how I believe I'm going to get to where I'm destined to go, even though I had to start over. And that's the risk. I took a temporary position. And it wasn't even something I wanted to do. But I knew I had to work.

PB: *And can you describe the nature of the job?*

RC: Well, I've been networking since I've been here (in St. Louis) and a gentleman said, "My father has a non-profit called Better Family Life." They do a lot of community work, which is what I want to do. I want to work with youth and in the community. So he said, "I'll pass your resume along." I had seen him at different United

Way events, and he asked, "Has anyone contacted you?" And I'm like, "No, no …" And so about a month and a half ago, someone called and said, "We got your resume and we have a position—a teen pregnancy prevention educator. And I was thinking in my mind, "Teen Pregnancy Prevention Educator?!" I really don't want to do that either! (laughs) And I'm sure it doesn't pay! But I went in for the interview, and I was impressed with the organization. And they said, "It's temporary, but there are so many opportunities that you can make your own way here." And I had applied for another job I really preferred—a program manager with the well-respected Wyman Group. And the Boys & Girls Clubs here didn't have anything at the time. So I said, "Better Family Life, this is where I need to be for the moment." So even though I made it to the final rounds of the interviewing with the other agency, I called them and said I'm taking this position. Even though it pays less than the other position and it's temporary.

So I'm in as the teen pregnancy prevention education director, and I'm called by the division manager into her office to talk about another position with workforce investment. They want me to work under the director as her right-hand man, so to speak. A Placement and Retention Specialist. To do compliance and placement, and to supervise at least two of her employees. And so I feel myself going to where I feel I'm destined to go—or at least I will pick up the skills I need to start my own non-profit in the future or to manage one.

I'm starting to see the pieces of the puzzle that, sometimes when you're Playing Big, you may have just one piece to the puzzle. But you just know that there are other pieces out there, and they're going to come together. And that's hard to do, because in this economy, people are playing it safe. Saying, "Stay in my job. I know I have dreams and visions, but my family needs to be fed." But if you feel destiny calling, you have to step out there. Because otherwise, you'll live below your potential. And that's one of my fears—that I won't live up to my potential.

I told my wife before we moved here, "I've got no job prospects." My fear is that I was going to end up being a manager at Burger King somewhere. And I was making almost six figures in D.C. At that job, I had a lot of contacts, I knew almost everyone. Now I'm coming to St. Louis, where I don't know anyone. You must know someone to get ahead here in St. Louis. But I didn't let that stop me. I could have said, "Let's stay in D.C. at the same job." But you feel destiny calling. And there were even some moments when I was a little depressed. It's been six or seven months and I'm still not working, but I just have to believe that it is all going to come together. You have to pursue your destiny. You can't just sit back and wait for it to come to you. You have to pursue it. You have to prepare.

PB: *When we started this interview, you stressed the importance of mentorship. I'm wondering, if you were to mentor a kid who resembled you at age 8 or 9, and in the kind of situation you came out of, how would you encourage them?*

RC: Well actually, I'm a Big Brother in Big Brothers & Big Sisters, and I've been a youth minister. So usually I tell my young people this: the choices you make today will determine the options that are available to you tomorrow. If you make bad decisions today, you are going to have bad options later. So if you drop out of high school, then when you want to work, you're going to have some bad options, like maybe McDonald's or Burger King. Not bad jobs if you're the manager or franchise owner, but if you're on the grill or the fry station, not so much! (laughs)

You don't always get to decide what happens to you, but you get to decide how you're going to react to what happens to you. I could have been mad, bitter, upset or angry at the world. Believed that someone owed me something, that the government owes me something, that my parents should have done this or should have done that. I had to erase all of that, and make the best decision I could with whatever resources I had at the time. It's all about making the best decision. Be forward thinking. Thinking, "If I'm 15 today, and I want to be a business owner in 10 years, I need to live for tomorrow, not today. I need to align myself with the right people and make better decisions as it pertains to my education, my character development, my health and wellness, my spiritual awareness—all of those things, I need to make holistic decisions about my life."

When a young person does that, when they take their life into their own hands, they realize, "I can't blame anyone but me." Or "Yes, my parents were born into poverty and now I'm poor, but what am I going to do to get out of poverty?" And, "If most of my family only have high school diplomas and I want a bachelor's degree, a master's degree or a doctorate, what can I do to get there?" And the resources are out there. But will they make the right decision? It also involves delayed gratification. I teach them that you have to deny yourself some pleasures—if it's having sex, if it's doing drugs, drinking, playing video games, watching TV—whatever it is, if you have to deny yourself those things to get ahead, you need to do it. Because you're going to pay now, or you're going to pay later. I think you should suffer now, so you don't have to suffer later, because eventually you're going to suffer. For the athlete, it's a lot of discipline, hurt, pain, sweat, tears and practice—but there's a reward later. That's what I try to instill in my young people. And sometimes they don't get it. But life will teach them. It's that African proverb, "If they won't listen to you, life will teach them." And to just believe in themselves—that they can do it. You can beat the odds—you don't have to be a statistic. Just look at me!

PB: *Yeah, really! Just look at you.*

EPILOGUE

"There Must Be Elephants ..."

"All shall be well, and all shall be well and all manner of things shall be well."

Julian of Norwich

AUTHOR'S NOTE: I delayed the publication of Playing Big so I could include this tribute to my friend, the late, great Bob Ginn. More than anyone I've ever known, Bob embodied the concept of Playing Big in his life. He did it all from a wheelchair, without the use of his arms or legs.

WHEN JULIAN OF NORWICH penned that quote back in the 15th century, she could not have imagined its fulfillment in the life of one man more than five hundred years later. That man was Bob Ginn. His life became, for me, a profound story of life, death and, ultimately, rebirth.

At 23, Bob had everything ahead of him. He was a gifted student about to begin his second year of law school. Then one sunny summer afternoon, while waterskiing, he hit a sandbar. The impact hurled him through the air some distance and he landed in shallow water on his head, breaking his neck. In the hospital following the accident, Bob's father took one look at his son's condition and quipped, "There goes a brilliant career."

The accident had left Bob paralyzed. He would never regain the use of his arms or legs. It became clear, however, that Bob wasn't giving up. He underwent 18 months of daunting rehabilitation before returning to law school. Unable to write, he dictated his class notes and his exams. He became an editor of the school's *Law Review*. Upon graduation, he was hired by a nationally recognized firm, where he practiced law for more than 10 years.

Bob is a shining example of Playing Big in its most enlightened and mature sense. What he accomplished in his lifetime would be impressive for anyone without his challenges. He worked with Legal Aid following his law firm tenure. Then he went back to school and earned two master's degrees (one in Theology and the other in Christian Spirituality), ultimately teaching Christian Spirituality at a university level. He became an advocate for the contemplative prayer movement. Bob travelled to Bora Bora *twice*—in a wheelchair. By choosing to Play Big in every moment every day of his life, he accomplished remarkable things, all from a place of his own disadvantage.

Bob also wrote a book about his experience that he called *A Brilliant Career*, after his father's remark in the hospital. I've often thought how brilliant that book title is. Prior to his accident, Bob was on track toward the popular notion of career and success. At the moment he became paralyzed, all his previous expectations of success had seemingly ended.When he learned to function as a quadriplegic, he regained success—graduating in the top ten of his law school class and landing a job with a prestigious law firm. He fulfilled all of his early promise of succeeding in a traditional American career, but eventually he found that it just wasn't enough. Ultimately, the book title reflects the transcendent nature of his journey. Bob realized that true success in life is measured in how much you give, not get. In the end, he would count those efforts to help others as his finest hours.

One of the biggest lessons I learned from Bob is that running away from your life is a losing strategy. He remarkably found a way to acknowledge the reality of his condition and have fun anyway. He'd lost his two front teeth to an errant baseball when he was a kid, and loved to dislodge his partial dental work and flash a toothless smile whenever the situation got grim. Fun was not merely an option. Bob insisted on it.

I saw Bob shortly before he passed away. Together, we'd organized a meditation group that met at his house for an hour each Saturday morning. The format was simple: three gongs followed by 30 minutes of silent meditation, then three more gongs and another 30 minutes of silence. We called it the Gong Show.

Bob had been very sick during the past nine months. Every day brought another acute medical problem. Most recently, it was his blood pressure. Between the hours of four and seven each day, his blood pressure had been shooting up into the stratosphere, raising grave concerns that he might have a stroke. When I saw him that Saturday morning, I asked about his blood pressure. He looked me straight in the eye, and with the impish grin of a young boy, he joyfully replied, "I don't care."

Looking back at that moment, I realize that Bob knew what was going to happen, and he really *didn't* care. He had died many times since his accident. His heart had stopped, breathing stopped. In each of these deaths, Bob had the experience we hear so much about: the tunnel, walking into the light, being greeted by the community. He told me once that he was far more confident about the hereafter than he ever was about this life.

Even before his paralyzing accident, Bob had dreamed about how he would leave this world. He was definitely from the Busby Berkeley school of funeral planning. The more pageantry, the better. Air thick to a state of opacity with incense. And elephants. Gloriously festooned pachyderms in an endless procession to the family plot.

We buried Bob Ginn with all the pomp and circumstance we could muster. Sadly, there were no elephants. At that point, however, the elephants seemed immaterial as we recounted all the things Bob had successfully manifested in his brief, big life. We also knew that somewhere in that hereafter Bob had glimpsed while he was still with us, there were elephants galore. And Bob, having now cast off his chair, was leading the herd.